Sewing Vintage Linens

Samantha McNesby

Published by

krause publications
An F&W Publications Company

700 E. State St.
Iola, WI 54990-0001
Telephone 715-445-2214
www.krause.com

Please call or write for our free catalog of publications. Our toll-free number to place an order or obtain a free catalog is 800-258-0929 or please use our regular business telephone, 715-445-2214.

Library of Congress Catalog Number: 2003101357

ISBN: 0-87349-532-2

Printed in the United States of America

The following registered or trademarked company or product names appear in this book: Americana® by DecoArt™, Cover Buttons kit by Prym®, Fabri-Tac Glue, Fire King, Gem-Tac Glue, Tulip Iron-on Transfer Paper for Color Copiers by Duncan, Tulip Iron-on Transfer Paper for Inkjet Printers by Duncan, Walnut Hollow, Weathered Wood® by DecoArt™

Editor: Barbara Case
Designer: Donna Mummery
Photos by Bobby Dalto, Photographics, Myrtle Beach, South Carolina.
Auction photos shot on location at C&C Auctions in Georgetown, South Carolina.

Acknowledgments

Writing a book is a daunting process – having a baby and writing a book at the same time is even more of a challenge! (See baby Sarah in several of the project photos in this book.) I am incredibly grateful to all of the folks who helped me pull this project together:

Thank you to the wonderful people at Krause Publications for making this dream a reality – Julie, Barbara, and Kris. I am so thankful for your guidance and your patience with my "first-timer" questions.

Joining the Society of Craft Designers was one of the best career decisions I have ever made! Many thanks to all of the talented designer and industry members for your advice and support. Special thanks to Lorine and Debra for your friendship and encouragement.

Many thanks are due to Pat Roman and the staff at Island Threads for always having just the right fabric, technique, or suggestion when a project hit a snag. Pat expertly quilted two of the projects in this book, and saved me countless hours of stitching time.

The beautiful photos were done by Bobby Dalto of Photographics. Thanks so much for understanding my "vision" and for always being willing to snap one more shot.

I am very lucky to have a large, creative, and supportive extended family! Thanks to all of you for always cheering me on, whatever I do. Thanks especially to my mom and dad for believing I can do whatever I set my mind to, and to my sister Emma for the many hours spent babysitting our new arrival.

My husband Jeff is so incredibly helpful and sweet about all of the projects I do! There is no way this book would have been completed without his help. He pitched in with everything – from talking about the idea of a book to hauling huge loads to and from the photo shoots, and everything in between – and I am very grateful.

Our daughter Sarah was born halfway through the writing of this book and accompanied us on photo shoots and shopping expeditions and kept me company at work in my studio. How lucky and blessed we are to have such a great little girl!

Baby Sarah.

Contents

Introduction

This book is meant to be source of inspiration, ideas, and actual projects for the home crafter or quilter. As collecting, displaying, and decorating with handwork and textiles have become more prevalent, "perfect" vintage textiles have become much more difficult to find. Chances are, when you are able to locate a perfect piece, it will be extremely expensive. However, less-than-perfect pieces of vintage embroidery, clothing, doilies, quilts, and coverlets are very easy to find and are much less expensive than their mint condition counterparts. Vintage pieces have also stood the test of time, and so are very durable. Frequent laundering has made these pieces luxuriously soft, and fading and minor flaws only add to their charm.

Part of the fun of working with vintage pieces is shopping! Check out the shopping guide in Chapter 1 for suggestions on selecting, purchasing, and caring for vintage linens. Come along for a visit to an auction, and learn the best techniques for scouting a flea market.

The projects featured in this book are designed to work together, and can be adapted to suit many different styles of vintage linens. The projects range in complexity from very simple, such as the handkerchief sachets, scrap tassels, and ornaments, to more complex, like the memory quilts, upholstered ottoman, and handkerchief footstool.

You will find the projects divided into four sections – those using embroidered accessories and handkerchiefs, those using "cutter" quilts and sheets, those using memory items including photographs and clothing, and those using scraps and bits of vintage pieces. Each section features projects ranging from fast and easy to more complex and time-consuming, so you can choose a project based on the time and vintage pieces available. Match a project to the linens you have on hand, gather your supplies, and jump right in! You will be living with and enjoying your linens in no time.

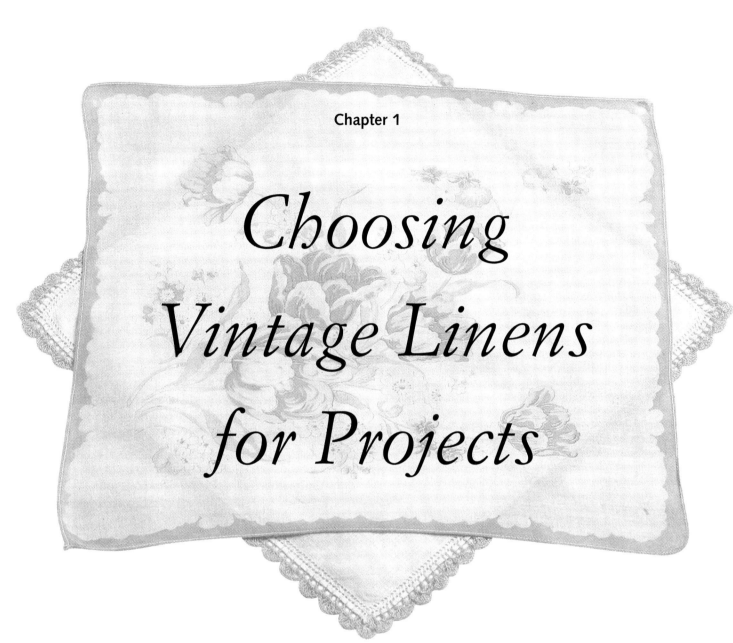

Chapter 1

Choosing Vintage Linens for Projects

Selecting Vintage Linens

Part of the fun of working with vintage linens is selecting just the right pieces for a project. I like to maintain a stash of linens in my studio. That way, when I am ready to work on a project, I have the right items on hand. Most of the items I use are one-of-a-kind, so it is difficult to go out and purchase to order. I generally have to buy an item when I see it and save it until I need it.

Although there has been more demand in the last few years, finding vintage linens is still relatively easy. Even with the increase in popularity, less-than-perfect linens can still be purchased at reasonable prices from a variety of sources. Keep your eyes open for any vintage textile – quilts, pillowcases, dresser scarves, table runners, doilies, dishtowels, handkerchiefs, and so much more. Women from generations past did a lot of handwork, so there's a nice variety to choose from.

What to Look For

Look for items in fair-to-good overall condition. Examine the piece carefully and check for stains, yellowing, or tears. You should also smell any piece you are considering buying. Some odors, like the slight mustiness of storage, will come out. Others, like smoke and mildew, will not. If the item is in less-than-perfect condition, look for salvageable areas. Small stains and tears on a handkerchief render it unusable, but the same small tears and stains on a bedspread leave plenty of usable material for crafting and sewing projects.

Don't be distracted by perceived flaws like incomplete trim or missing buttons. You won't be using these pieces as-is, and their less-than-perfect condition allows you to cut into them without guilt (and to purchase them at great savings).

What to Avoid

Your eyes and nose are your best tools to determine what to avoid – stains, smoke, and mildew are the most common culprits with old linens. Be sure to give everything a thorough examination. Completely unfold any item you are interested in purchasing. Minor flaws can be worked around but you need to check the whole piece to be sure it is in usable condition.

If you have a chance to handle the item, crush the fabric lightly in your fingers. If it crackles at all, don't purchase it. Give it a sniff. Smoke, water, and mildew odors are next to impossible to get out.

Avoid items that are damaged beyond repair, either by age, poor storage, bad odors, staining, or major flaws in embroidery.

Watch out for linens that have been excessively starched. They may feel crisp when you purchase them, but starching can make the fibers brittle and too fragile to work with. Items that smell of bleach may be a very bright white but often retain the bleach smell after repeated washings. Heavy use of bleach also damages the fibers, often resulting in damage when the fabric is washed or exposed to sunlight.

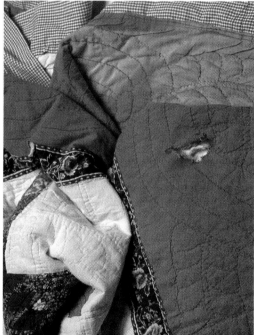

This quilt is a wonderful candidate for projects. The center of the quilt is intact and in good condition and could be used as-is for a large project or cut into pieces for smaller ones. This quilt is considered to be of "craft" or "cutter" quality because of the fading and tears in the border. Turn to page 63 to see how this quilt was used on an ottoman.

I also avoid using true antiques or collector's items. Save these for display to accent your creations. Not only are antique or collectible-quality pieces expensive, they are usually too beautiful to cut into. There are so many less-than-perfect items out there, I prefer not to cut into an item that is in collectible condition. This is a personal preference, so if you find the "perfect" pieces for your project and don't mind the extra expense, go for it!

Although many less-than-attractive linens are salvageable, true "uglies" should be avoided. Unusable items include linens with ugly or harsh colors, awful fabrics, lumpy texture, huge, unattractive patterns, and fabrics that feel terrible to the touch. If you don't like the initial piece – its color, texture, embroidery, etc. – you won't like the finished project either!

It is sometimes hard to decide which piece to start with. These are often one-of-a-kind items, so some reluctance to cut into a piece is normal. Don't work with pieces you don't care for just because you don't want to wreck the "good" stuff.

This quilt has sustained too much damage to be used for new projects. The fabric has disintegrated in many areas and is dry and brittle in others.

I like to plan my projects out before I cut into any fabric. The pieces I work with are often one-of-a-kind, so I want to be sure that an idea will work before I begin.

Printed hand-kerchiefs come in a variety of colors and patterns.

A 1940s child's hankie is pressed and ready to be used in a project.

A delicate hand-embroidered handkerchief, a souvenir hankie from Buckingham Palace, and a pretty lace-trimmed bride's hankie spill from a vintage change purse.

Handkerchiefs

Hankies are great for making smaller projects or for adding a splash of color to larger ones. Handkerchiefs come in a huge variety of colors and styles. They can be embroidered by hand or machine, printed with floral or other patterns, or trimmed with crocheted or lace edges. Children's and souvenir hankies are also available, but are prized by collectors so they are often more expensive than regular styles.

When you shop for handkerchiefs, look for pretty, clean pieces in colors you like. While a perfect crocheted or lace edge is nice and gives you more options, hankies with imperfect edges can often be used for sewing projects.

Be on the lookout for sets or singles. Sets of three to four hankies can sometimes be found in the original packaging. If you see a handkerchief with your initial, or the initial of someone close to you, buy it! These will come in handy when you need to add a personal touch to a project.

Hankies are still a great bargain. I have spent anywhere from $.25 to $5 on a single handkerchief, depending on the quality and how much I liked it. Buying hankies in a "lot" at auction often yields a lower per-piece price.

What luck! When I opened this vintage canister bought at a local auction, I discovered three perfectly matched red and ivory handkerchiefs inside. I used the red hankies for the pillow project on page 42.

These complete sets of handkerchiefs were a great find. They are shown here in their original boxes.

I used this set of table decorations to make the sewing accessories on page 27.

Southern belle pillowcases are a favorite of many collectors. The skirt can be made from lace, as pictured here, appliquéd fabric, or crocheted trim. I used this pillowcase for the covered hanger project on page 40.

You will find a variety of motifs on embroidered table runners and pillowcases.

Embroidered Accessories

In the past, it was fairly common to embroider items like placemats, table runners, pillowcases, and napkins for home décor. These pieces almost always feature "pretty" images like flowers, animals, and monograms, and will add a great handmade touch to your vintage linen projects. They can be used for small-to-medium sized projects or to add a special touch to larger ones.

Embroidered accessories can be purchased in groups or as single items. Buy embroidered accessories in matching groups if you are planning a quilt or a series of items that match. If you are working on a single project, like a pretty accent pillow or accessory, a single piece is all you need.

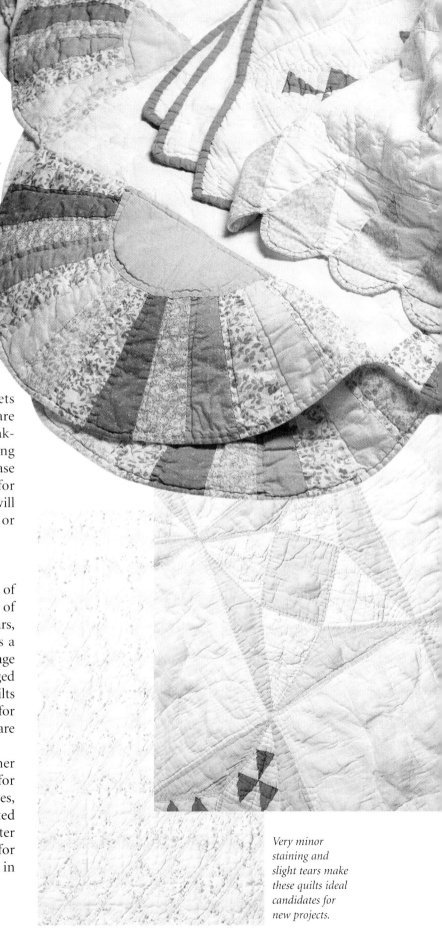

"Cutter" Quilts, Bedspreads, and Sheets

The term "cutter" applies to quilts and other large textiles that are too damaged to use for their original purpose but still have salvageable areas. By cutting around the damaged areas, you can use portions of the quilt for craft projects like the ones featured in this book.

Quilts, bedspreads, and bed sheets work well for any sized project. They are large enough for covering furniture, making or backing new quilts, or creating matched sets of items. When you purchase these items, check the entire surface for flaws. Most cutter or craft quality items will have some flaws, usually small tears or stains you can work around.

Quilts

Making a quilt takes a huge amount of time and commitment. Sadly, the art of quilting was unappreciated for many years, and multitudes of great quilts suffered as a result. Poor treatment, inadequate storage methods, and shoddy care have damaged many quilts beyond repair. While quilts damaged in this manner may be unusable for the originally intended purpose, they are perfect for crafting.

Damaged (cutter) quilts are sold either whole, in pieces, or as tops only. Look for cutter quilts at independent quilt stores, quilt shows, or at one of the venues listed later in this chapter. Most of the cutter quilts in my collection were purchased for under $50 and large scraps can be found in the $10 to $20 range from most sources.

Very minor staining and slight tears make these quilts ideal candidates for new projects.

These orphan blocks were easy to date – they were pieced on pages from a 1946 magazine.

This raspberry pink chenille bedspread is one of my favorite finds. It is in excellent condition and I was thrilled to purchase it at auction for only $15.

"Orphan" quilt blocks can also be found from a wide variety of sources. Orphan blocks are single quilt blocks, or a small set of quilt blocks that were never incorporated into a larger project. The original quilt maker may have decided not to complete the project, or may have had leftover blocks when she was finished. Either way, the resulting blocks, or orphans, work great for smaller projects.

Bedspreads

Bedspreads are wonderful to work with. They provide a great quantity of fabric for a minimal price. I prefer to purchase either vintage cotton printed spreads or cotton chenille spreads. A full-sized chenille bedspread in craft condition will yield about four yards of fabric for about $20 (about $5 per yard). New chenille of the same quality is about $25 per yard – a substantial difference in price!

Sheets and Pillowcases

Vintage sheets and pillowcases are usually soft cottons, often with pretty vintage floral patterns or ticking stripes. Sheets and pillowcases are great for a variety of projects – especially when soft, draping fabric is a must. Use a pretty vintage sheet as a backing for a quilt or as the lining for a jacket. Expect to pay under $3 each for sheets and pillowcases in good condition. Many of the sheets in my collection were purchased for under $1 each.

These baby dresses feature delicate embroidery and crisp, smooth fabric.

Clothing

Vintage clothing works well for a variety of projects. Clothing items are especially suited to memory projects. Use "special" items such as baby clothing, flannel shirts, ties, scraps of dresses and aprons, and even t-shirts to personalize your projects. Don't forget pretty details – lace and embroidered collars and cuffs, pretty buttons, smocked dress fronts, etc. Use special clothing pieces from your own family or snip accessories from vintage finds.

Where to Find Vintage Linens

Vintage textiles can be found in a variety of settings. Look for old linens in your own home, antique stores, flea markets, and auctions. If you have Internet access, you can even purchase linens online, through auctions and web stores. My favorite places to look for vintage linens are listed below, along with tips for shopping and purchasing at each venue.

Your Own Home

Surprisingly, one of the best places to look for vintage textiles is in your own home. Check

This lace collar made a pretty addition to the memory quilt project on page 97.

the attic, the garage, the top shelf of the linen closet, and those drawers you rarely open. Chances are you have a few usable pieces on hand. Usually these items are in your home for one of two reasons – either you purchased them because you liked them or you received them as a gift or inheritance. Either way, making a project allows you to enjoy these items rather than stashing them away in a forgotten drawer.

Family and Friends

Let your family and friends know that you are looking for linens to use for your projects and you may be surprised at what turns up! Your friends and family may have some items you can use, or they can look for vintage linens as they shop. Some of my favorite pieces came from family and friends who saw something they thought I could use when they were shopping for other items.

Antique and Consignment Stores

Antique stores, antique malls, and consignment shops often carry assortments of vintage textiles. Usually the linens found in these venues are in good-to-perfect condition and are priced accordingly, but you can occasionally find some bargains. Even if you pay a bit more for a "perfect" item from a consignment or antique shop, by making your own finished project, you will still pay considerably less than you would in a retail, gallery, or designer setting, and the piece will be uniquely yours.

When shopping in antique or consignment stores, look for dealers who don't normally handle linens, but have a few to sell. They will generally offer better prices. Look for incomplete sets or imperfect items, or "lots" of unrelated items (several items in the same bag or box for a single price). Linens packaged this way will often be more reasonable. Don't overlook single napkins, gloves, bags of trims, etc. Look in drawers, boxes, and tins – you never know what is tucked away! Let the store owner know what you are looking for. Sometimes they have less-than-perfect items stashed away from the sales floor and will be more than happy to sell them to you.

Gather everything you are interested in purchasing, whether it is two items or 20, and make a single bid to the store owner. At worst they will say no, at best they will give you a discount. Asking for a 10% to 15% discount is not offensive, and often expected.

Flea Markets

Flea markets are great places to look for old textiles. Linens, clothing, and household items are often sold at very reasonable prices, especially if they are in less-than-perfect condition. Look for sellers who are only there for the day. Established dealers often have higher prices. Homeowners selling at the flea market for a single day or weekend hoping to unload a few items generally have better prices. These sellers are there to get rid of things and make a few dollars, not to run a business.

Garage and Yard Sales

Shopping at garage and yard sales is very similar to shopping at flea markets, with a few exceptions. To get the best selection, you must get an early start. Most garage and yard sales are over by noon. As important as getting an early start is to never show up before the posted hours of the garage sale. Arriving just in time or a minute or two early is acceptable, but showing up at a private home at 5:00 a.m. for a 7:00 a.m. garage sale is not.

Unlike a flea market, a garage sale often has many buyers looking over (and in competition for) the same merchandise. There are no other booths to distract shoppers, so if you see something you think you want to purchase, pick it up and carry it while you decide. I have missed out on great pieces because I decided I wanted something, only to find it had sold while I finished looking over the rest of the merchandise.

Auctions

Auctions are one of the best sources for finding vintage linens. They can be a bit intimidating for the first time bidder, so do some homework before you attend your first one. Check for auction houses in the phone book or look for auction announcements in your local newspaper. They are usually listed near the garage sale classifieds. Be sure to show up early. Most auctions offer several hours of preview time so you can look at the items up for bid. Auctions are "no-return" shopping venues, so be sure to check the merchandise carefully before you bid.

When calculating how much you want to spend for an item, remember that a buyer's premium will often be added to the price. This additional fee is usually a percentage of the sale price and is added when you cash out at the end of the auction. Be sure to ask about buyer's premiums, as they can add up.

Most auction houses sell a variety of merchandise – everything from estate and consignment items to store closeouts and overstocks to

Tips for
Flea Market Success

1. Arrive early! Sellers arrive and set up before the posted start time, and so should you. Arrive early and move quickly for the best selection. If you see something early in the day, make an offer or purchase it outright if you really love it. If your offer is not accepted, check back before you leave because prices often drop as the day wears on and most sellers don't like to pack things up and bring them home.

2. Dress in layers. Most flea markets are held outdoors and almost always start early in the morning. An outfit that is comfortably warm at 7:00 a.m. may be uncomfortably hot by 10:30. Be ready to shed layers as needed for comfort.

3. Bring a snack. While there are always exceptions, the food available at flea markets is iffy at best, and can be downright scary at worst. Come prepared with a light snack to munch as you shop.

4. Bring small bills and change. Flea market prices are usually inexpensive and you won't want to miss a great bargain because the vendor doesn't have change for a large bill. (Plus, it is awfully fun to be able to purchase a great piece for actual pocket change!)

5. Bring a large tote bag or a carryall with wheels to tote all of your finds. Unlike a traditional store, flea market vendors don't usually have bags or other items to make toting your purchases easy. Leave a sturdy box and a few newspapers in the car for wrapping any fragile items for the trip home.

6. Bring a truck. Drive your own or borrow one if you are interested in furniture finds. Flea markets are cash-and-carry businesses, so be prepared to carry your purchases home.

7. Be prepared. Bring a tape measure if you are looking for items for specific projects or to fit odd-sized areas of your home. Bring a magnifying glass or reading glasses if you collect items with maker's marks like pottery or silver. Know the measurements of your doorways and stairwells if you are looking for large furniture pieces. Some older pieces are larger and wider than contemporary doorways can handle, so it is better to know in advance if that "perfect" armoire will fit through the front door of your home.

8. Think creatively. Look at items in new ways. For linens, ask yourself if you can use them for current or future projects. Do they match items you already have on hand? For furniture, can you use the hardware, drawers, or trim for other projects? Use mismatched silver on your table, or bend it to use for hooks or curtain tiebacks.

9. Negotiate! Offer a lower price on any item you are interested in. Some negotiation is expected and is part of the fun of flea market shopping. When you are interested in several items from a single seller, gather everything you are interested in purchasing and make a single bid. The worst that can happen is that the seller turns you down, but they may give you a discount.

10. Remember, an item is not yours until you have paid for it. If you see something you are considering buying but want to look over the rest of the seller's merchandise first, pick the item up and hold it, if possible. Other buyers are looking at the same merchandise, and if the item is in your hands, you are not likely to lose it to another buyer. Disagreements do crop up between potential buyers over who "saw it first." If the item in question is in your hands, you are less likely to lose out on a great piece.

This auction featured a wide variety of items including furniture, china, glassware, vintage jewelry, and vintage linens.

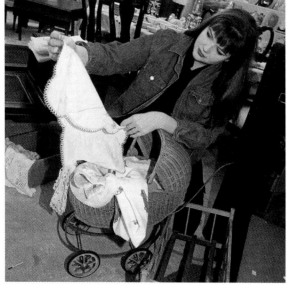

Always read the auction rules, as they vary from place to place. At C&C Auctions, they post them right on the wall.

plain old "junk." There is often no discernible logic to the order of items placed on the auction block. Occasionally, items are offered in numerical order by lot number. This is most often the case in estate and high-end auctions where the items are also featured in a catalog.

Bidding

At even the most rustic of country auctions, you will need to register. You will be asked to provide some basic information to the auctioneer's office and will receive information about the auction itself, either in written form or posted on the wall. If you have a question, ask! The successful completion of the sale is as important to the auction house as it is to you. Be sure you know what forms of payment the auction house accepts and what the terms of sale are.

When you register you will be assigned a number. Most auctions give each bidder a paddle with their number on it to use when bidding. Contrary to popular belief, you won't be credited for a bid if you move your hands about or stand up while bidding is going on. You should, however, refrain from waving your hands wildly in the air if you are not bidding.

Top, before you bid, be sure to check the merchandise carefully. Bottom, when bidding, hold your paddle in the air so the auctioneer can see your number.

Once you have registered, find a seat on the bidding floor. Listen carefully to the auctioneer. He will let you know what you are bidding on. This information should include a description of the item, including its physical appearance, any markings, the item's approximate age if known, and its provenance or heritage if known. A good auctioneer will point out flaws, but not all do. Many flaws are subjective, so hopefully you will have checked out the merchandise first. The auctioneer has the final say over the winning bid and who bought the item.

The auctioneer explains how many items are up for bid. When more than one item is presented (three quilts, for example), the auctioneer will tell you how the items will be sold. If the quilts are being sold as one lot, the auctioneer will take bids and sell the group for the highest bid. If the quilts are being sold as individual items, the highest bidder will get first choice of the quilts. The winning bidder may choose to take one, two, or all three, and the winning bid is the price for each one. If the winner only wants one quilt, the remaining quilts are offered to the floor for another round of bidding until they are sold.

The auctioneer offers an opening bid and lets you know if there is a reserve price, which is the lowest price the seller will accept. If the reserve price is not met, the item is not sold, regardless of the highest bid. Not all items have reserve prices.

Be sure to have an idea of the maximum amount you are willing to spend on an item and stick to it. It is easy to get caught up in "auction fever" and bid more than you intended. Keep in mind that a buyer's premium and taxes may be added to your final bid.

Online Auctions

Online auctions follow the same general rules as live auctions. One of the great benefits of using an online auction service is the ability to search thousands of listings for specific items at your convenience.

Online auctions run continuously and you can see a wide selection of items, often offered at competitive prices. Since you don't need to be present at the auction to bid, you can purchase items from across the country or around the world. Items in demand in your region can sometimes be found at greatly reduced prices when purchased from another area. The largest and most user-friendly online auction house is ebay.com, but other auction houses are available on the Internet.

Tips for
Successful Bidding

☞ As the auctioneer opens the bid, don't jump in right away. Often, if the first amount he calls out isn't accepted, the opening price will drop. The lower the opening bid, the lower the final cost may be. It is not unusual to get a lot consisting of several items for a low price, sometimes under $5.

☞ Speed is not essential in bidding. The auctioneer will always give a warning before closing the sale. Take your time as you bid and keep track of how much you are bidding.

☞ Avoid getting into a competitive bidding war with another bidder. If you are determined to "win," you will almost certainly end up paying too much for an item. Be willing to walk away. Some items will go higher than your maximum amount. Remember, an item isn't yours until you have won the final bid.

☞ Bring a light snack and beverage and perhaps something to read. Auctions can run for a long time. Anywhere from two to six hours is average, depending on the speed of the auctioneer, size of the crowd, and number of items up for bid.

☞ Keep track of your winning bids by lot number and amount as you go. This record will give you a pretty accurate total of your expenditures and purchases at any time. A small notebook is helpful for taking notes on prospective items and for recording your purchases. If your bidder paddle is paper, you can jot down this information on the back of it.

Common Online Auction Terms

Seller: The person selling the object. The seller lists the object for sale with a written description and usually a photo. When you purchase items through an online auction, payment is made to the individual seller, not to the auction house, so if you buy three separate items, you will need to make three separate payments.

Feedback: Both sellers and bidders have feedback ratings. Auction users rate one another based on their purchasing experiences. Each online auction service is different, so be sure to check the rules before you bid.

Minimum bid: Determined by the seller, this is the starting bid that will open the auction.

Reserve price: The seller can choose to set a reserve price. Just like at a live auction, an item will not sell unless the highest bid meets or exceeds the reserve price.

Bidding Online

You will need to have a computer and access to the Internet to participate in an online auction. Visit the auction site and browse around. You generally will not need to register until you decide to place a bid. If an item offered for auction appeals to you and you want to place a bid, you will need to register. Follow the online prompts to register and be sure to read the auction site's rules and terms. If the auction site has a bidder's tutorial (most large ones do), take a moment to view it. Once you have registered, you will only need to enter your name and password to place bids. The auction site will retain the rest of your information.

Once you have registered, you can start bidding. Use the "search" feature to see auctions for specific items. Try searching for "vintage linens," "handkerchiefs," or "quilts" and look over the huge number of items for sale in each of these categories. Carefully review a listing before placing a bid. Make sure you know what the item is, its condition, shipping cost, and terms of sale, including how the seller wishes to be paid. Always check the feedback rating of the seller before placing a bid.

When you have won an auction, the seller will contact you to arrange payment and shipping services. Never place a bid on an item if you don't intend to follow through. As in a traditional auction, sellers are charged a fee based on sales.

Placing bids without paying for the items will also result in negative feedback and many online services won't allow you to participate after you receive a few negatives.

Cleaning and Caring for Your Purchase

Once you have purchased your vintage linens, you will need to clean and store them until you are ready to use them. Whenever I make a new purchase, I clean the item right away, then place it with my other vintage pieces. This way, all the linens I have are ready to work with when I need them.

When you bring a new piece home, try to determine what fabric it is, if possible, and treat the piece accordingly. Evaluate the current condition of each piece by checking the stitching, embroidery, and trim. Decide whether the piece should be hand or machine washed, and pre-treat any stained areas. Remember how you washed each piece. If an item survives the first trip through the washer, your finished project will too. If a piece is damaged while you are cleaning it, it is better that the damage occurs before you put time and effort into a project.

Most of the linens I have on hand are either cotton or linen and can be machine washed. Keep in mind that most of the vintage linens suitable for use in projects have survived for decades without special care.

Store your linens clean and ready to use. If you wash everything as it comes in, all your vintage pieces will be ready to work with when you need them. Fold large pieces like quilts, bedspreads, and sheets and store them on a shelf away from direct sunlight. Clothing of all sizes can be stored on hangers until ready to use. Small pieces and trims can go in plastic or cardboard storage bins. I sort my smaller items by type, keeping handkerchiefs in a pretty vintage hankie box, ties in a plastic storage bin, and buttons in a clear glass apothecary jar. Whatever storage method you use, be sure to store all your linens and trims away from direct sunlight, pets, and moisture.

Chapter 2

Embroidered Accessory & Handkerchief Projects

The projects in this chapter are made from a variety of vintage linens, including small embroidered doilies, pillowcases, table runners, and handkerchiefs. While your linens will not exactly match the ones shown, use the projects as a guide for selecting pieces to work with.

Decorative Pillows

Embroidered linens of all shapes and sizes make
wonderful pillow fronts. Accent your linens with coordinating
fabrics and fluffy chenille. These decorative pillows were
made from a table
runner and an
embroidered
tea towel.

Pink Pillow

Directions

Note: This project uses a ¼" seam allowance.

1 Cut the fabrics.

From the white chenille cut:
19½" x 19½" square
(2) 4" x 12½" strips
(2) 4" x 19½" strips

From the pink cotton cut:
10½" x 10½" square

From the blue cotton cut:
(2) 1½" x 10½" strips
(2) 1½" x 12½" strips

2 Place the square of pink cotton right-side-up on your work surface. Spray the back of the crocheted-edge table runner with fabric basting spray and carefully center it on top of the pink cotton. The tip of the table runner should be about 2" from the edge of the pink fabric. Stitch it in place, then use scissors to trim away the rest of the table runner.

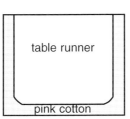

3 Add the blue border: Place the table runner piece on a flat work surface with the right side up. Place a 1½" x 10½" blue strip along the top and bottom. Stitch in place, keeping the right sides together and the edges aligned. Press. Repeat with the 1½" x 12½" blue strips at the sides of the table runner piece.

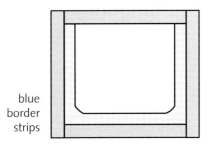

blue border strips

Vintage linens
* embroidered table runner with crocheted trim, 8" wide
* large white chenille scrap, at least 36" x 36"
* 2 yards of white chenille trim, 5" wide

Other fabrics and trims
* scrap of pink cotton, at least 12" x 12"
* ¼ yard of light blue cotton

Other supplies
* rotary cutter, ruler, and mat, or ruler, fabric marker, and scissors
* fabric basting spray
* pencil
* fiberfill
* needle and thread
* sewing machine and accessories (this project can be done by hand, but it will be more time-consuming)
* iron and pressing surface

4 Add the chenille border: Place the table runner piece on a flat work surface with the right side up. Place a 4" x 12½" chenille strip along the top and bottom. Stitch in place, keeping the right sides together and the edges aligned. Press. Repeat with the 4" x 19½" chenille strips at the sides of the table runner piece.

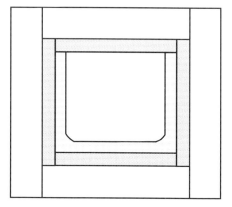

white chenille border strips

5 Place the completed pillow front right-side-up on your work surface. Place the chenille fringe on top of the pillow front, matching up the raw edges. The fringes should face the center of the pillow. Stitch in place.

6 Assemble: Place the pillow front and chenille back with the right sides together, lining up the edges. Stitch around the edges of the pillow, leaving an opening for turning and stuffing.

7 Turn and press. Stuff firmly with fiberfill and hand stitch the opening closed.

Yellow Pillow

Directions

Note: This project uses a ¼" seam allowance.

1 Cut the fabrics.

From the white chenille cut:
16½" x 16½" square
(2) 2½" x 12½" strips
(2) 2½" x 16½" strips

From the blue cotton cut:
(2) 1¼" x 8" strips
(2) 1¼" x 9½" strips

From the yellow ticking cut:
(2) 2" x 9½" strips
(2) 2" x 12½" strips

You will need:

Vintage linens
* embroidered tea towel
* large white chenille scrap, at least 36" x 36"
* 1½ yards of white chenille trim, 5" wide
* ¼ yard of yellow striped pillow ticking

Other fabrics and trims
* ¼ yard of light blue cotton
* 4 round white buttons, ¾" diameter

Other supplies
* rotary cutter, ruler, and mat, or ruler, fabric marker, and scissors
* fabric basting spray
* pencil
* fiberfill
* needle and thread
* sewing machine and accessories (this project can be done by hand, but it will be more time-consuming)
* iron and pressing surface

2 Measure and cut an 8" x 8" square from the embroidered tea towel, with the embroidered portion in the center of the square.

3 Add the blue border: Place the tea towel on a flat work surface with the right side up. Place a 1¼" x 8" blue strip along the top and bottom. Stitch in place, keeping the right sides together and the edges aligned. Press. Repeat with the 1¼" x 9½" blue strips at the sides of the tea towel.

4 Add the yellow border: Place the tea towel on a flat work surface with the right side up. Place a 2" x 9½" yellow strip along the top and bottom. Stitch in place, keeping the right sides together and the edges aligned. Press. Repeat with the 2" x 12½" yellow strips at the sides of the tea towel.

tea towel

5 Add the chenille border: Place the tea towel piece on a flat work surface with the right side up. Place a 2½" x 12½" chenille strip along the top and bottom. Stitch in place, keeping the right sides together and the edges aligned. Press. Repeat with the 2½" x 16½" chenille strips at the sides of the tea towel piece.

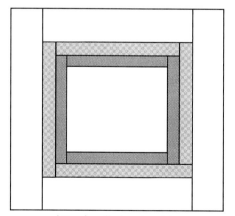

white chenille border strips

6 Place the completed pillow front right-side-up on your work surface. Place the chenille fringe on top of the pillow front, matching up the raw edges. The fringes should face the center of the pillow. Stitch in place.

7 Stitch a white button at the edge of the blue border at each corner.

8 Assemble: Place the pillow front and chenille back with the right sides together, lining up the edges. Stitch around the edges of the pillow, leaving an opening for turning and stuffing.

9 Turn and press. Stuff firmly with fiberfill and hand stitch the opening closed.

Sewing Accessories

This set of sewing accessories is fast and easy to make. I found the pretty embroidered table accessories used for this project at a local thrift shop for under $1.

Directions

Note: *These projects use a ¼" seam allowance.*
Note: *If your embroidered accessories don't have crocheted trim or the trim is damaged, substitute ½ yard of lace or the trim of your choice.*

Pincushion

1 Make a plastic template: Use a pencil to draw a 4" diameter circle on the plastic template sheet. (For a perfect circle, trace around a 4" coffee mug or can.) Cut out the template.

You will need:

Vintage linens
* 3-piece set of matching embroidered accessories with small (under 3") embroidered motifs and crocheted edges. The pieces I used were 8" x 12" each.

Other fabrics and trims
* 1 yard of white satin ribbon, ¼" wide
* 1 yard of pink satin ribbon, ⅛" wide
* 1 gold heart button, ½" wide
* white felt, 9" x 12" sheet
* pink felt, 9" x 12" sheet

Other supplies
* scissors
* clear plastic template sheet
* pencil
* ruler
* water-soluble fabric marker
* fiberfill
* needle and thread
* Gem-Tac Glue
* 1" foam brush
* sewing machine and accessories (this project can be done by hand, but it will be more time-consuming)
* iron and pressing surface

2 Cut the front and back: Place an embroidered accessory right-side-up on a flat work surface. Place the clear plastic circle template on top of the scrap. Move the template around until you are happy with the way the cut piece will look. Trace around the circle template with a water-soluble fabric marker. Use scissors to cut out the circle on the traced line. Mark and cut a circle of plain fabric for the back.

3 Cut the trim: Use scissors to cut the crocheted trim from the straight edges of the embroidered accessory, leaving a ¼" wide strip of fabric attached to the trim. Cut a 12" length of trim.

4 Attach the trim: Place the pincushion front right-side-up on your work surface. Place the trim on top of the pincushion front, matching up the cut edges. The crocheted edge should face inward. Stitch in place.

5 Assemble: Place the pincushion front and back with the right sides together, lining up the edges. Stitch around the edges of the pincushion, leaving an opening for turning and stuffing.

6 Turn and press. Stuff very firmly with fiberfill and hand stitch the opening closed.

Scissor Fob

1 Make a plastic template: Use a pencil and ruler to draw a 5" square on the plastic template sheet. Cut out the template.

2 Cut out the front and back: Place an embroidered accessory right-side-up on a flat work surface. Place the clear plastic square template on top of the scrap. Move the template around until you are happy with the way the cut piece will look. Trace around the template with a water-soluble fabric marker. Use scissors to cut out the square on the traced line. Mark and cut a square of plain fabric for the back.

3 Cut the trim: Use scissors to cut the crocheted trim from the straight edges of the embroidered accessory, leaving a ¼" wide strip of fabric attached to the trim. Cut a 5" length of trim.

4 Attach the trim: Place the scissor fob front right-side-up on your work surface. Place the trim at the bottom, matching up the cut edges. The crocheted edge should face inward. Stitch in place.

5 Assemble: Place the scissor fob front and back with the right sides together, lining up the edges. Stitch around the side and bottom edges, leaving the top open for turning and stuffing. Turn and press.

6 Hem the top edge by turning it under ¼". Press and stitch in place.

7 Cut an 18" length of ⅛" wide pink ribbon. Hold the ends of the ribbon together and tie a knot, forming a loop. Place the tied ends inside the scissor fob, allowing the loop end to extend out of the opening.

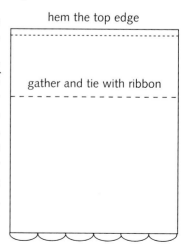

hem the top edge

gather and tie with ribbon

8 Stuff firmly with fiberfill, keeping the ribbon ends inside. Pinch the top opening closed and secure by tying it with the remaining 12" length of pink satin ribbon. Tie a bow and trim the ribbon ends with scissors.

Needle Book

1 Place an embroidered accessory piece on a flat work surface with the right side down. Use the foam brush to apply a light layer of Gem-Tac Glue to the back of the embroidered accessory. Apply the glue only to the fabric, avoiding the crocheted edges. Place the glued side down on top of a sheet of white felt, smoothing out any wrinkles. Let the glue dry.

2 Use scissors to trim the felt around the embroidered accessory. Cut along the fabric of the piece, allowing the trim to hang free.

3 Place the embroidered accessory on a flat work surface with the felt side up. Fold the accessory in half to form a "book" shape. Press. Open the book.

4 Place the 1 yard length of white ribbon across the inside of the needle book. Glue the ribbon in place and let the glue dry.

5 Cut a 4" x 7" strip of pink felt. Open the needle book and place the pink felt inside, referring to the photo for placement and centering it carefully. Glue the pink felt in place.

6 Close the needle book and tie the ribbon ends. Trim the ribbon tails as desired.

7 Hand stitch or glue the ½" gold heart button in place on the front of the needle book. To use, open the book and insert the needles in the pink felt.

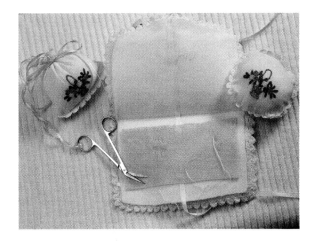

Covered Album

Make this pretty album to store your favorite photos.
The handkerchiefs shown here were part of a lot of pink linens,
purchased at an online auction.

Note: *The photo album shown is 8½" x 10½", a common size. If your album is a different size, you will need different amounts of fabric and batting. To custom fit your album, measure the open album cover. Cut the batting the same size as the album cover. Cut the cover fabric large enough to wrap easily around the edges of the album and proceed as directed.*

Directions

1 Before beginning, press all the fabrics and the batting to remove any wrinkles.

2 Remove the photo pages from the album. Cut a 10½" x 19" piece of cotton quilt batting. Place the batting on a flat work surface. Use the foam brush to apply a coat of Gem-Tac Glue to the outside cover of the album. Place the album cover-side-down on top of the cotton quilt batting. Be sure all the edges line up and smooth the batting in place. (You can reposition the batting as needed while the glue is wet.) Let the glue dry.

3 Cut an 11½" x 20" piece of the pillowcase. Place the pillowcase piece on a flat work surface with the right side down. Use the foam brush to apply Gem-Tac Glue to the spine of the album. Carefully center the spine of the album on the pillowcase. Open the album and double check the fit (there should be enough pillowcase fabric to wrap around all the edges). Add glue to the front and back cover of the album, smoothing the fabric in place as you work. Let the glue dry.

You will need:

Vintage linens
* white ladies handkerchief with pink floral print, 10" x 10"
* white handkerchief with pink floral embroidery, 10" x 10"
* white handkerchief with lace trim, 8" x 8"
* white pillowcase with embroidered trim

Other fabrics and trims
* ½ yard of white cotton quilt batting

Other supplies
* 8½" x 10½" ring-bound photo album (Don't worry if there's a design on the cover – you will cover it with fabric)
* black and white photo (I used a 2" x 3½" photo)
* rotary cutter and mat, or ruler, fabric marker, and scissors
* Gem-Tac Glue
* 1" foam brush
* iron and pressing surface

4 Place the album on a flat work surface with the cover side down. Fold down the excess pillowcase fabric at the top of the album and glue it in place on the inside cover. Let the glue dry. Fold up the excess fabric at the bottom of the album and glue it in place. Let the glue dry. Fold in the excess fabric at each side and glue it in place. Let the glue dry.

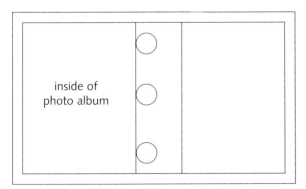

pillowcase

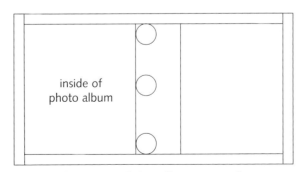

fold over and glue pillowcase to album

5 Place the pink floral handkerchief on a flat work surface and use a rotary cutter and ruler to cut it in half diagonally. Glue the handkerchief halves to the front of the photo album, referring to the photo for placement. Fold the top 1" of the handkerchief over to the inside of the album and glue it in place. Let the glue dry.

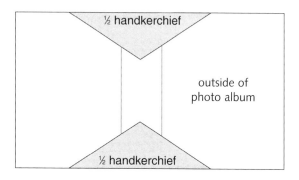

6 Cut a 7" x 10" piece of cotton quilt batting. Use the foam brush to coat the inside back cover of the album, including the pillowcase fabric edges, with Gem-Tac Glue. Carefully center the batting on top of the inside back cover. Let the glue dry.

7 Cut a 10" x 10" piece of cotton quilt batting. Use the foam brush to coat the inside front cover of the album, including the pillowcase fabric edges, with Gem-Tac Glue. Carefully center the batting on top of the inside back cover. Let the glue dry.

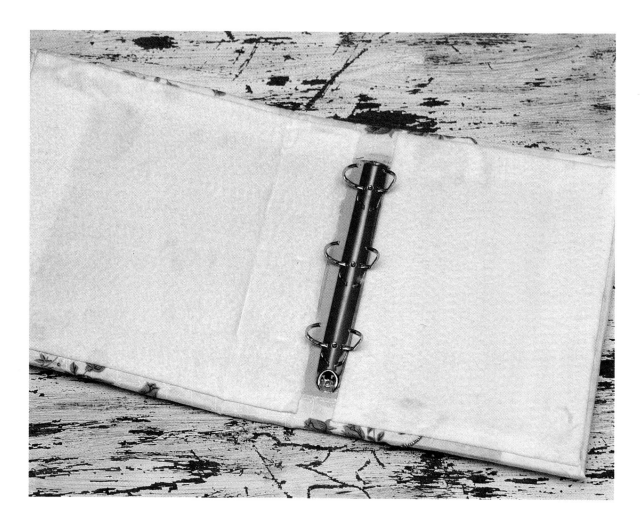

8 Place the embroidered handkerchief right-side-down on the pressing surface. With the embroidered motif facing you, fold the two side corners in until they meet. Press.

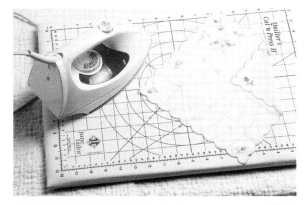

9 Fold the top of the handkerchief down. Press.

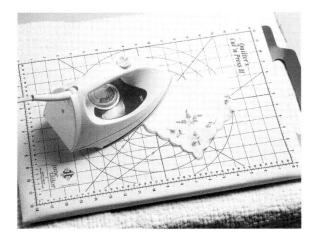

10 Glue the embroidered handkerchief to the front of the album, centering it carefully and gluing only the sides and bottom. Let the glue dry.

11 Replace the album pages. Tuck the white lace handkerchief and photo into the pocket.

Handkerchief Sachets

These sachets are fast and easy to make, and would be delightful favors for a bridal or baby shower.

Directions

1 Place the handkerchief right-side-down on your pressing surface. Iron to remove any wrinkles.

2 Center a handful of fiberfill on top of the handkerchief.

3 Add a few drops of fragrance or essential oil to the fiberfill.

4 Gather the handkerchief around the fiberfill and pinch the fabric together above the ball of fiberfill. Let the ends of the handkerchief hang free. Tie the 12" length of ribbon around the gathered fabric. Knot the ribbon to secure.

5 Use a hot glue gun to attach a white silk rose to the ribbon, covering the knot completely.

You will need:

Vintage linens
* printed ladies handkerchief, any size

Other fabrics and trims
* 12" length of white satin ribbon, ⅛" wide

Other supplies
* fiberfill
* essential oil or fragrance
* scissors
* hot glue gun and glue sticks
* white silk rose with leaves, 1½" diameter
* iron and pressing surface

Handkerchief Footstool

Show off the vibrant colors of a vintage floral handkerchief with this fun-to-make footstool project. I used the fringe from a chenille bedspread, but you can substitute new cotton fringe if you need to.

You will need:

Vintage linens
* red floral print ladies handkerchief, 12" x 12"
* large white chenille scrap, at least 24" x 24"

Other fabrics and trims
* ¼ yard of red cotton
* 1½ yards of white cotton 3" fringe

Other supplies
* pre-made wood footstool with 10" x 13" rectangle top
* acrylic craft paint in red and white (I used Calico Red and Warm White by DecoArt)
* 1-step crackle medium (I used Weathered Wood by DecoArt)

* white or ivory votive candle or tea light
* plastic palette knife
* matches
* 1" foam paintbrush
* 1" old scruffy paintbrush
* rotary cutter, ruler, and mat, or ruler, fabric marker, and scissors
* pencil
* 10" x 13" piece of 3" thick upholstery foam
* heavy-duty staple gun and staples
* hot glue gun and glue sticks
* sewing machine and accessories (this project can be done by hand, but it will be more time-consuming)
* iron and pressing surface

Directions

Note: This project uses a ¼" seam allowance.

Paint the Footstool

1 Use the foam brush to paint the legs and bottom of the footstool with white paint. Let dry. (This is a distressed finish, so there is no need to sand or seal the footstool before beginning.)

2 Light the candle and let it burn until there is a pool of wax around the wick. (Keep the candle level on a flat surface and never leave it burning unattended.)

3 Use the palette knife to scoop out a small amount of liquid wax. Use the flat side of the palette knife to apply liquid wax sparingly to the flat surfaces of the footstool legs and bottom. Apply the wax randomly to make small dimensional mounds or beads. Don't rub the wax in. These little bumps create a resist for the red paint you will apply later.

Note: When applying wax, concentrate on areas that would normally get the most wear, such as the edges and corners.

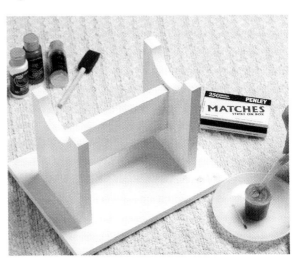

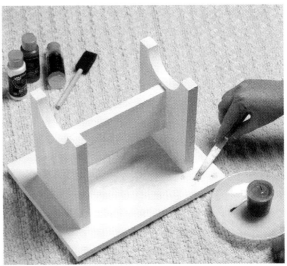

4 Use the foam brush to apply a small amount of crackle medium to the legs and bottom of the footstool. Let dry.

5 Use the foam paintbrush to apply red paint to the legs and bottom of the footstool. Paint with a full brush, using a pouncing motion. Completely cover the white basecoat. Let dry. The paint will crackle as it dries.

6 Carefully peel away the bumps of wax from all surfaces of the footstool. Your fingernails are the best tools for removing the wax, which should come off easily. If you have difficulty with the wax, put the footstool in the freezer for a few minutes, then try again.

This finish simulates the look of old, peeling paint.

Make the Cover

1 Cut the fabrics.

From the red cotton cut:
(2) 1½" x 12" strips
(2) 1½" x 15" strips

From the white chenille cut:
(2) 4" x 15" strips
(2) 4" x 23" strips

2 Add the red border: Place the handkerchief right-side-up on a flat work surface. Place a 1½" x 12" red strip along the top and at the bottom of the handkerchief. Stitch in place, keeping the right sides together and the edges aligned. Press. Trim the edges if needed. Repeat with the 1½" x 15" red strips at the sides of the handkerchief.

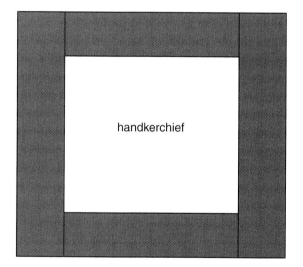

3 Add the chenille border: Place the handkerchief piece on a flat work surface, with the right side up. Place a 4" x 15" chenille strip at the top and at the bottom of the handkerchief piece. Stitch in place, keeping the right sides together and the edges aligned. Press. Trim the edges if needed. Repeat with the 4" x 23" chenille strips at the sides of the handkerchief piece.

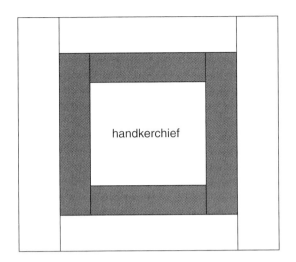

Assemble the Footstool

1 Place the footstool on your work surface. Position the upholstery foam on the top and glue it in place. Let the glue dry.

2 Press the handkerchief piece to remove any wrinkles. Place the handkerchief piece right-side-down on your work surface. Carefully center the footstool with the foam side down on top of the fabric.

3 Starting on one long side, pull the chenille border over the edge of the wood and staple it in place. Starting from the center, work your way to each corner, pulling the fabric taut. Repeat for the other long side, pulling the chenille firmly as you work so the fabric will lay flat on top of the foam.

4 Working on a short side, fold the chenille "gift wrap" style and staple it in place. Repeat for the other short side.

5 Add the fringe: Use the glue gun to attach the fringe around the edges of the footstool. Let the glue dry completely.

Southern Belle Pillowcase Hanger

Pillowcases featuring southern belles are among my favorites. The pillowcases I used for this fast and simple project were damaged beyond repair, but the embroidery was still in good condition. Make a set of these ultra-feminine hangers as a gift or use them in your own closet.

Directions

Note: This project uses a ¼" seam allowance.

1 Working in a well ventilated area, paint the hook portion of the wire hanger with white or ivory spray paint. Let the paint dry.

Make the Batting Lining

1 Place the cotton quilt batting on a flat work surface. Place the wire hanger on top of the batting. Use the water-soluble marker to trace around the top and sides of the hanger. Don't trace around the hook. Remove the hanger from the quilt batting. Use a ruler and the water-soluble marker to add 3" to the bottom of the hanger pattern. Mark directly on the quilt batting.

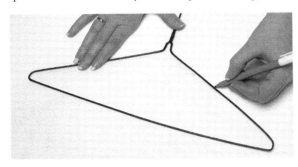

2 Place the unmarked scrap of quilt batting on a flat work surface. Top with the marked scrap of quilt batting. Stitch the pieces together on the marked line, leaving the bottom open and a ½" opening at the top for the hanger hook.

3 Use scissors to trim away the excess batting ¼" from the seam. Snip the seam allowance along the curved edges. Trim the bottom along the marked line. Turn and press.

4 Insert the hanger hook through the small opening at the top of the lining.

You will need:

Vintage linens
* embroidered pillowcase with southern belle motif

Other fabrics and trims
* 2 scraps of cotton quilt batting, at least 12" x 18" each

Other supplies
* wire hanger
* white or ivory satin finish spray paint
* scissors
* ruler
* water-soluble fabric marker
* sewing machine and accessories (this project can be done by hand, but it will be more time-consuming)
* iron and pressing surface

Make the Cover

1 Turn the southern belle pillowcase inside out. Place the pillowcase on a flat work surface. Place the batting-covered wire hanger on top of the pillowcase. Move the hanger around until you are satisfied with the placement. The pillowcase should cover the batting completely. Use the water-soluble marker to trace around the top and sides of the hanger. Do not trace around the hook.

2 Remove the hanger from the pillowcase. Stitch the pillowcase together on the marked line, leaving the bottom open and a ½" opening at the top for the hanger hook.

3 Use scissors to trim away the excess fabric ¼" from the seam. Do not trim the bottom. Turn and press.

4 Insert the hanger hook through the small opening at the top of the pillowcase cover.

Handkerchief Pillows

These pillows are the perfect way to show off your prettiest printed hankies. Try the soft pink version for a romantic look in the bedroom, or make the bold red version for the porch or family room.

Pink Pillow

Directions:

Note: *This project uses a ¼" seam allowance.*

1 Measure and cut one 18" square from the pink gingham fabric and one 18" square from the white chenille fabric.

2 Place the square of pink gingham right-side-up on your work surface. Spray the back of the crocheted-edge handkerchief with fabric basting spray and carefully center it on top of the gingham. Stitch in place.

3 Spray the back of the printed handkerchief with fabric basting spray and carefully center it on top of the crocheted-edge handkerchief. Stitch in place.

4 Place the completed pillow front right-side-up on your work surface. Place the chenille fringe on top of the pillow front, matching up the raw edges. The fringes should face the center of the pillow. Stitch in place.

5 Assemble: Place the pillow front and chenille back with the right sides together, lining up the edges. Stitch around the edges of the pillow, leaving an opening for turning and stuffing.

You will need:

Vintage linens
* linen handkerchief with pink crocheted trim, 12" x 12"
* cotton handkerchief with pink floral print, 12" x 12"
* pink gingham pillowcase, or ½ yard of jumbo pink gingham
* large white chenille scrap, at least 18" x 18"
* 2 yards of white chenille trim, 5" wide

Other supplies
* rotary cutter, ruler, and mat, or ruler, fabric marker, and scissors
* fabric basting spray
* pencil
* fiberfill
* needle and thread
* sewing machine and accessories (this project can be done by hand, but it will be more time-consuming)
* iron and pressing surface

6 Turn and press. Stuff firmly with fiberfill and hand stitch the opening closed.

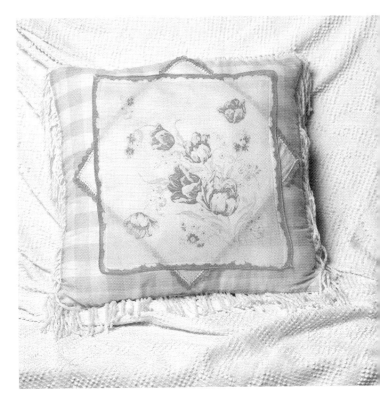

You will need:

Vintage linens
* handkerchief with red floral print, 12" x 12"
* handkerchief with red geometric print, 10" x 10"

Other fabrics and trims
* ½ yard of red and white polka dot cotton
* 2 yards of ball fringe

Other supplies
* rotary cutter, ruler, and mat, or ruler, fabric marker, and scissors
* fabric basting spray
* pencil
* fiberfill
* needle and thread
* sewing machine and accessories (this project can be done by hand, but it will be more time-consuming)
* iron and pressing surface

Red Pillow

Directions

Note: *This project uses a ¼" seam allowance.*

1 Measure and cut two 18" squares from the red polka dot fabric.

2 Place a square of red polka dot fabric right-side-up on your work surface. Spray the back of the floral print handkerchief with fabric basting spray and carefully center it on top of the red polka dot fabric. Stitch in place.

3 Spray the back of the red geometric handkerchief with fabric basting spray and carefully center it on top of the floral print handkerchief. Stitch in place.

4 Place the completed pillow front right-side-up on your work surface. Place the ball fringe on top of the pillow front, matching up the raw edges. The fringe should face the center of the pillow. Stitch in place.

5 Assemble: Place the pillow front and back with the right sides together, lining up the edges. Stitch around the edges of the pillow, leaving an opening for turning and stuffing.

6 Turn and press. Stuff firmly with fiberfill and hand stitch the opening closed.

Pillowcase Dress

This project is both fun and functional. Use an old pair of bib overalls and a pretty vintage pillowcase to make a sweet new dress for your favorite little girl. Give her a chance to play fashion designer by letting her select a pretty pillowcase "skirt." This project works best for sizes 6 and under.

You will need:

Vintage linens
* embroidered pillowcase with lace trim

Other fabrics and trims
* 24" length of pink cotton belting, 1" wide

Other supplies
* pair of child's size denim bib overalls
Note: When complete, this project is worn by pulling the overalls over the child's head. Be sure the overalls you choose are large enough to fit over the head comfortably.
* scissors
* measuring tape
* water-soluble marker
* needle and thread to match the pillowcase
* 3 hook-and-loop tape circles, 1" diameter
* hot glue gun and glue sticks
* 3 silk roses with leaves, 1½" diameter
* pins
* sewing machine and accessories
* iron and pressing surface

Directions

1 Use scissors to cut away the bottom portion of the overalls, just below the bib.

2 Measure the skirt length: Place the bib portion of the overalls over the child's head. Measure from the bottom of the overall bib to the desired hem length (the sample is just below the calf). Add 1" to this measurement. The skirt in the photo is 21" long.

The embroidery on the pillowcase makes for a darling design on the skirt.

3 Cut the pillowcase: Measure and mark the skirt length on the pillowcase. Cut across the pillowcase on the marked line.

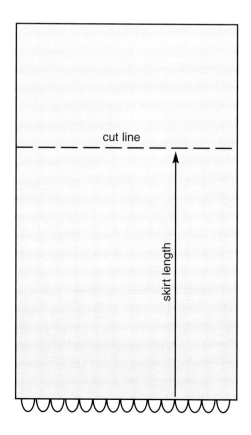

4 Thread the needle and sew ½" gathering stitches around the top of the pillowcase. Gather to fit the overalls.

5 With right sides together, pin the gathered pillowcase to the overalls, lining up the cut edges. Stitch in place. Press.

6 Place the pink belting over the seam and stitch it in place.

7 Stitch the hook portion of one of the hook-and-loop tape circles to the center of the overall bib.

Repeat for the other two circles, positioning them about 1" apart.

The roses are detachable so the dress can be washed.

9 Add the roses to the front of the overalls by reattaching the hook-and-loop tape circles.

8 Use the hot glue gun to attach a loop portion of the hook-and-loop tape to the back of each silk rose. Let the glue cool.

10 To wear, pull the dress over the child's head. When it's time to wash the dress, remove the roses and reattach them afterwards.

Even the littlest girls can wear a pillowcase dress. Use baby-sized overalls and omit the flowers for safety reasons.

Upholstered Seat Chair

Cheerful raspberry chenille and a delicate vintage table runner give this old chair a great new look. I used a folding chair, but you can substitute other types as long as the back of the chair is open.

Note: This project uses a recycled chair with a 17" x 17" seat. If your chair seat is a different size, you will need different amounts of chenille fabric and a different size pillow form. To custom fit your chair, measure the seat. Use a pillow form the same size or slightly larger. Cut the chenille fabric large enough to wrap easily around the chair seat and proceed as directed.

Directions

This chair was unattractive, but in very good condition. By adding a fresh coat of paint and a few vintage linens, the chair is now suitable for any room in your home.

Paint the Chair

1 Use the foam brush to paint the chair black. Let the paint dry. (This is a distressed finish, so there is no need to sand or seal the chair before beginning.)

2 Rub the flat side of the candle all over the chair, focusing on the areas that would get the most natural wear. Rubbing the candle will leave a light coat of wax on the painted wood surface. The wax will create a resist for the top coat of paint.

You will need:

Vintage linens
* embroidered table runner, 12" x 36"
* large raspberry chenille scrap, at least 24" x 24"

Other fabrics and trims
* 3 gold and pearl buttons, assorted shapes, ½" diameter
* 2 white buttons, ⅜" diameter

Other supplies
* wood folding chair
* pre-made pillow form, 18" x 18"
* acrylic craft paint in black and ivory (I used Lamp Black and Buttermilk by DecoArt)
* white or ivory votive candle
* rotary cutter, ruler, and mat, or ruler, fabric marker, and scissors
* pencil
* 1" foam paintbrush
* 1" old scruffy paintbrush
* medium sandpaper
* heavy-duty staple gun and staples
* hot glue gun and glue sticks
* sewing machine and accessories (this project can be done by hand, but it will be more time-consuming)
* iron and pressing surface

3 Use the scruffy brush to apply two coats of ivory, letting the paint dry between coats. Let the chair dry overnight to give the paint a chance to "cure" completely before proceeding.

4 Rub all surfaces of the chair with the medium grit sandpaper. The paint will come off easily where the wax resist was applied, allowing the basecoat to show through.

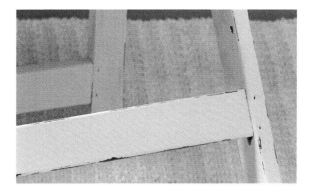

Make the Cover

1 Cut the table runner in half. Center half of the table runner on the raspberry chenille, lining up the cut edges. Stitch in place, then press to remove any wrinkles.

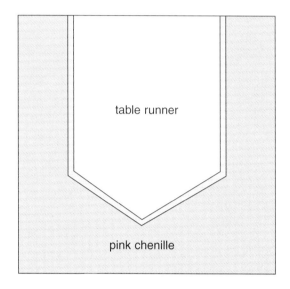

2 Place the chair on your work surface. Place the pillow form on the chair seat.

3 Place the chenille cover on top of the pillow form. Starting at the back, pull the chenille over the edge of the seat and staple it in place on the bottom of the chair. Starting from the center, work your way to each corner, pulling the fabric taut as you work. Repeat for the front, pulling the chenille firmly as you work so the fabric will lay flat on top of the pillow form.

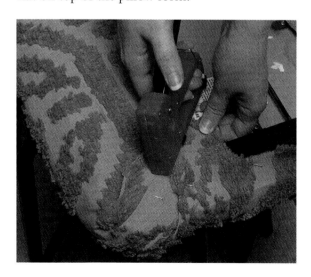

4 Pull the chenille over one side of the chair and staple it in place on the bottom. Repeat for the other side. If your chair has side supports, pull the chenille fabric around them and staple it in place on the bottom of the chair.

5 Hot glue a gold and pearl button to the point of the table runner. Glue a round white button to each side of the table runner. Let the glue cool before using.

6 Stitch a gold and pearl button to each side of the remaining table runner half.

7 Drape the table runner half over the back of the chair. Experiment with the placement, then hot glue the fabric to the back of the chair, letting the point of the table runner hang over the front of the chair.

Chapter 3

Cutter Quilt

&

Sheet

Projects

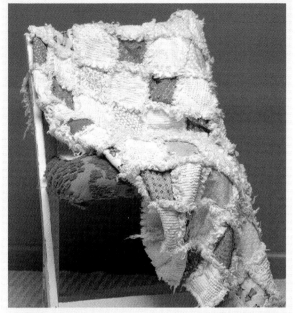

The projects in this chapter are made from old quilts, sheets, and bedspreads. Make a small accent like the Hanging Heart Pillow, or create a whole room outdoors with the Garden Party projects. Either way, cutter quilts, sheets, and bedspreads make wonderful source materials for projects.

Project #10: Hanging Heart Pillow
Project #11: Quilt Angel
Project #12: Hatboxes
Project #13: Memory Board
Project #14: Quilt Ottoman
Project #15: Scottie-Shaped Pillow
Project #16: Chenille Baby Quilt
Project #17: Special Occasion
                 Chair Cover
Project #18: Garden Tea Party

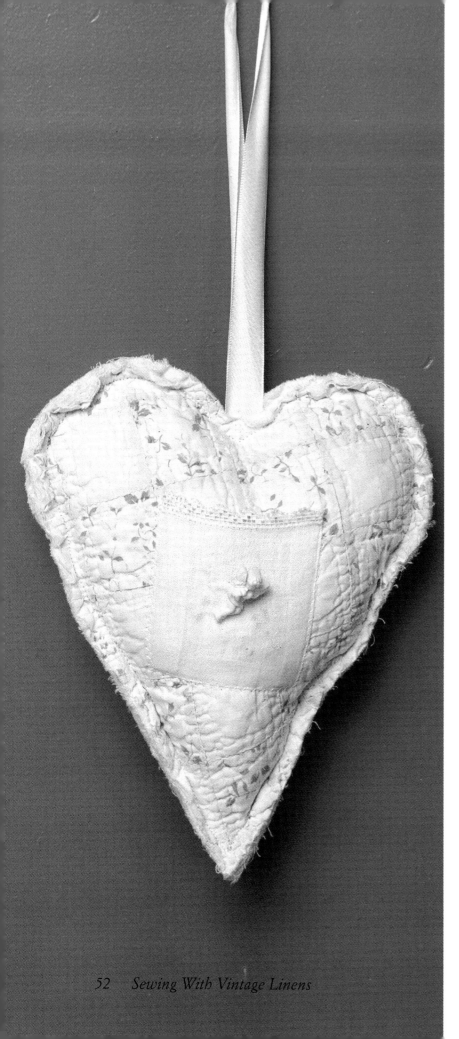

Hanging Heart Pillow

Use small quilt scraps to make a charming heart to hang from a door or on the wall. The exposed seams and tiny pocket give it a simple, primitive flair.

Directions

Note: This project uses a ¼" seam allowance.

1 Make a plastic template: Use a pencil to trace the heart pattern from page 121 onto the clear plastic template sheet. Cut out the heart template.

2 Cut out two fabric hearts: Place a cutter quilt scrap right-side-up on a flat work surface. Place the plastic heart template on top of the scrap. Move the template around until you are happy with the way the cut piece will look. (Experiment with different areas of the quilt until you find the one you like.) Trace around the heart template with a water-soluble fabric marker. Repeat, for a total of two hearts.

3 To make the pocket, cut a 3" x 3" square from the ladies handkerchief. Cut the square from the edge of the handkerchief so that one side will have the embroidered trim. This will be the top of the pocket.

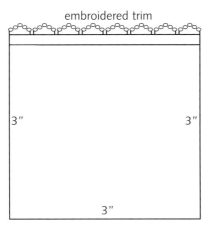

4 Place the 3" x 3" square right-side-down on a flat work surface. Turn the bottom of the pocket up ½" and press. Repeat for the two sides, but not the top.

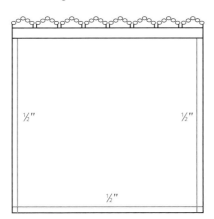

5 Attach the pocket: Decide which of the two quilt hearts will be the front of the pillow. Carefully center the cherub button on the front of the pocket and stitch it in place. Carefully center the pocket on the *front* quilt heart and hand stitch it to the heart.

6 Add the hanger: Fold the 16" length of ivory satin ribbon in half with one end on top of the other. Place the pillow back right-side-down on a flat work surface. Carefully center the dou-

You will need:

Vintage linens
* 2 cutter quilt scraps, at least 7" x 9" each
* ladies hankie with crocheted trim, any size

Other fabrics and trims
* 16" of ivory satin ribbon, ⅝" wide
* plastic cherub button, 1" diameter

Other supplies
* scissors
* clear plastic template sheet
* pencil
* water-soluble fabric marker
* fiberfill
* needle and thread
* sewing machine and accessories (this project can be done by hand, but it will be more time-consuming)

bled length of ribbon at the top of the heart. About 1" of the ribbon tails should lay on the heart, the rest should form a loop hanger. Stitch the ribbon to the pillow back.

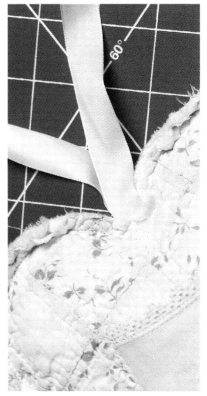

7 Assemble the pillow: Place the pillow back right-side-down on a flat work surface. Place the pillow front right-side-up on top of the back. Topstitch around the edges of the pillow with a ¼" seam allowance. Leave a 3" opening for stuffing. Stuff firmly with fiberfill and topstitch the opening closed.

Quilt Angel

Use this quilt angel as a doll, or display her on a bed or table. I cut her dress and wings from quilt scraps and made her body from a vintage sheet and trims.

Directions

Note: *This project uses a ¼" seam allowance.*

1 Make the plastic templates: Use a pencil to trace the angel body, wing, and dress patterns from pages 122 and 123 on the clear plastic template sheet. Cut out the templates.

2 Cut out two dress and two wing pieces: Place a quilt scrap right-side-up on a flat work surface. Place the clear plastic dress template on top of the scrap. Move the template around until you are happy with the way the cut piece will look. (Experiment with different areas of the quilt until you find the one you like.) Trace around the dress template with a water-soluble fabric marker. Cut out two dress pieces. Use the same technique to cut out two wing pieces.

3 Cut out the body: Place a sheet scrap right-side-up on your work surface. Top with a second scrap, right-side-down. Place the clear plastic body template on top of the scraps. Trace around the body template with a water-soluble fabric marker. Cut out the two body pieces.

4 Place the body pieces with right sides together and sew all the way around, leaving a 3" opening for turning. Turn the body right side out and press. Stuff firmly with fiberfill and hand stitch the opening closed.

5 Place the dress pieces with right sides together and sew the shoulders and sides of the dress. Leave the neck, sleeves, and bottom of the dress open. Turn the dress right side out and press.

6 Dress the angel by pulling the dress over her head, and her arms through the sleeves.

7 Use a hot glue gun to add the trims. Wrap the ivory satin ribbon around the waist and glue the ribbon ends in place at the back of the body. Glue the pink rosette to the ivory ribbon at the front of the body. Wrap the string pearls around the neck and glue the ends in place at the back of the neck to secure. Wrap the upholstery fringe across the top of the head, following the curve, and glue it in place.

You will need:

Vintage linens
* 2 cutter quilt scraps for the dress, at least 10" x 10" each
* cutter quilt scrap for the wings, at least 6" x 8"
* 2 ivory or white cutter sheet scraps for the body, at least 8" x 8" each

Other fabrics and trims
* 8" length of ivory satin ribbon, ⅝" wide
* pink satin rosette, ½" diameter
* 8" length of ivory plastic string pearls, ⅛" wide
* 4" length of upholstery fringe, 2" wide

Other supplies
* scissors
* clear plastic template sheet
* pencil
* water-soluble fabric marker
* fiberfill
* needle and thread
* hot glue gun and glue sticks
* sewing machine and accessories (this project can be done by hand, but it will be more time-consuming)
* iron and pressing surface

8 Place the wings right-side-up on a flat work surface. Place the angel on top of the wings. When you are happy with the wing placement, hot glue them to the body.

Hatboxes

Use these handy round boxes to store everything from photographs and mementos to costume jewelry and accessories. The blue vintage sheet I used to cover these boxes was a great auction find.

Fabric-Covered Box

Note: *The fringe and fabric requirements for this project are based on a 12" x 6" round box. If your box is a different size, you will need to adjust the fabric measurements accordingly.*

You will need:

Vintage linens
* blue floral sheet piece, at least 8" x 40"
* large ivory tablecloth or drapery scrap, at least 16" x 16"

Other fabrics and trims
* 40" length of ivory fringe, 3" wide

Other supplies
* paper mache round box with lid, 12" diameter x 6" tall
* 4 wood candle cups, 1¾" tall
* acrylic craft paint in ivory (I used Buttermilk by DecoArt)
* 1" flat brush
* rotary cutter and mat, or ruler and scissors
* scissors
* water-soluble fabric marker
* Gem-Tac Glue
* plastic or foam plate
* 12 hinge-style clothespins

Directions

1 Cover the box: Cut an 8" x 40" strip from the blue floral sheet. Pour glue on a plastic or foam plate. Use the 1" flat brush to apply glue to the outside of the round box. Work on a 4" to 6" section at a time, pressing the fabric in place as you go. Allow the fabric to overlap the top and bottom by 1". Let the glue dry.

2 Use scissors to make slits in the excess fabric around the bottom of the box. Snip the fabric every 2", right up to the edge of the box. Place the box on a flat work surface with the bottom facing you. Fold the excess fabric over the bottom of the box and glue it in place. Let the glue dry.

3 Use scissors to make slits in the 1" of excess fabric around the top of the box. Snip the fabric every 2", right up to the edge of the box. Fold the excess fabric to the inside of the box and glue it in place. Let the glue dry.

4 Add the feet: Use the 1" flat brush to paint the outside of the candle cups with ivory. Place the box on a flat work surface with the bottom facing you. Position the four candle cups with the openings up. Glue the candle cups in place. Let the glue dry.

5 Cover the lid: Use a foam brush to apply glue to the top of the box lid. Carefully center the ivory tablecloth scrap on top of the lid, smoothing out the fabric with your fingers. Let the glue dry.

6 Place the lid with the fabric side down on a flat work surface. Use the fabric marker and ruler to mark off a circle 1¼" from the edge of the lid. Cut the fabric on the marked line. Use scissors to snip the fabric every 2", right up to the edge of the lid. Fold the snipped fabric over the sides of the lid and glue it in place. Let the glue dry.

7 Attach the fringe: Glue the fringe around the sides of the lid. Hold the fringe in place with clothespins until the glue dries.

You will need:

Vintage linens
* blue floral sheet scrap, at least 16" x 16"

Other fabrics and trims
* 40" length of ivory fringe, 3" wide

Other supplies
* paper mache round box with lid, 12" diameter x 6" tall
* 4 wood doll heads, 1½" diameter
* acrylic craft paint in blue and ivory (I used Chiffon Blue and Buttermilk by DecoArt)
* 1-step crackle medium (I used Weathered Wood by DecoArt)
* 1" foam brush
* 1" flat brush
* Gem-Tac Glue
* scissors
* water-soluble fabric marker
* plastic or foam plate
* 12 hinge-style clothespins

Painted Box

Note: *The fringe and fabric requirements for this project are based on a 12" x 6" round box. If your box is a different size, you will need to adjust the fabric measurements accordingly.*

Directions

1 Paint the box: Use the foam brush to basecoat the outside of the box and the doll heads with blue acrylic paint. Let the paint dry.

2 Use the foam brush to add a coat of crackle medium to the outside of the box and the doll heads. Let dry.

3 On the plastic or foam plate, mix a small amount of water with some ivory paint. Use just enough water to thin the paint slightly, about one part water to five parts paint. Use the 1" flat brush to apply this mixture to the outside of the box and the doll heads. Let the paint dry.

4 Add the feet: Place the box on a flat work surface with the bottom facing you. Glue the doll heads in place. Let the glue dry.

5 Cover the lid: Use a foam brush to apply glue to the top of the box lid. Carefully center the blue floral sheet scrap on top of the lid, smoothing out the fabric with your fingers. Let the glue dry.

6 Place the lid with the fabric side down on a flat work surface. Use the fabric marker and ruler to mark off a circle 1¼" from the edge of the lid. Cut the fabric on the marked line. Use scissors to snip the fabric every 2", right up to the edge of the lid. Fold the snipped fabric over the sides of the lid and glue it in place. Let the glue dry.

7 Attach the fringe: Glue the fringe around the sides of the lid. Hold the fringe in place with clothespins until the glue dries.

Memory Board

Display photos and special mementos on this attractive, easy-to-make memory board. For my memory board I used plastic, metal, and glass buttons snipped from vintage garments.

Note: I used a recycled frame with a 12" x 16" opening. If your frame is a different size, you will need different amounts of fabric, batting, and foam core. To custom fit your frame, measure the frame opening. Cut the foam core and batting ¼" smaller than the frame opening. This will allow the memory board to fit into the frame snugly after it has been wrapped with fabric. Cut your fabric and strips large enough to wrap easily around the board.

Directions

1 Paint the frame: Use the foam brush to basecoat the frame with white paint. Let the paint dry. Add a second coat if needed (if your frame has a dark finish, two coats may be needed).

2 Place the foam core on a flat work surface. Top with the quilt batting and glue it in place using Gem-Tac Glue. Let the glue dry.

3 Press the fabric to remove any wrinkles. Place the fabric right-side-down on your work surface. Carefully center the foam core piece, batting-side-down, on top of the fabric. Use scissors to trim the fabric around all the sides, leaving at least 3" of fabric on each side.

You will need:

Vintage linens
* cutter bedspread or tablecloth scrap, at least 16" x 20"

Other fabrics and trims
* 4 yards of ivory satin ribbon, ⅜" wide
* 8 green vintage buttons, assorted styles, ½" to ¾"

Other supplies
* 18" x 22" wood frame with a 12" x 16" opening (recycled or new)
* satin finish paint in white (I used Soft White Americana Satin by DecoArt)
* rotary cutter, ruler, and mat, or ruler and scissors
* scissors
* 1" foam paintbrush
* ¼" foam core, cut to 11¾" x 15¾"
* quilt batting, cut to 11¾" x 15¾"
* light-duty staple gun
* Gem-Tac Glue
* iron and pressing surface

4 Starting at the top, pull the fabric over the edge of the foam core board and staple it in place. Start at the center and work your way to each corner, pulling the fabric taut as you work. Repeat for the bottom, pulling the fabric firmly as you work so the fabric lays flat on the front of the board. Working on a side, fold the fabric "gift wrap" style and staple it in place. Repeat for the other side.

5 Add the ribbons: Cut eight 18" lengths of ⅜" wide ivory satin ribbon. Place one ribbon piece diagonally across the front of the memory board (from the top center of the board to the lower corner). Wrap one end of the ribbon around the back of the board and staple it in place. Repeat for the other end. Trim any extra ribbon with scissors.

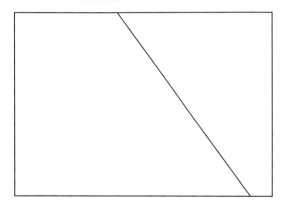

6 Add the remaining ribbons to the board in the same manner. Ribbons should be placed 5" apart and should form an "X" where they intersect.

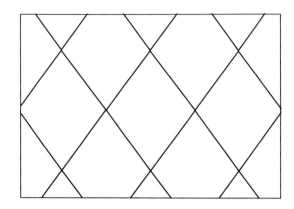

7 Where the ribbons cross, use Gem-Tac Glue to secure the ribbons to the fabric. Let dry.

8 Use scissors to snip the shanks from the vintage buttons (if they have shanks). Use Gem-Tac Glue to glue a button to each ribbon intersection. Let the glue dry.

9 Insert the covered foam piece into the frame. Add a 1" sawtooth hanger to the back of the frame, if needed.

The memory board will hold photos, postcards, and a variety of mementos.

Quilt Ottoman

Using a drawer as the base for this project allows you to make a "real" piece of furniture without investing a lot of time or money. Each drawer will vary in size, so measure yours carefully before you begin. I chose the paint colors to accent the quilt.

You will need:

Vintage linens
* cutter quilt or large quilt scrap
* vintage sheet to match the quilt

Other supplies
* medium/large dresser drawer
* 4" thick upholstery foam, cut to fit the drawer opening (available at home décor and craft stores)
* ½" thick plywood, cut to fit the drawer opening
* 4 ball fence post screw-on finials, 6" tall (in the fence section of the hardware store)
* 3 wood flower medallions, 3" diameter or large enough to cover holes left by removing standard dresser hardware (I used #16023 by Walnut Hollow)
* 4 wood blocks, 2" wide
* acrylic craft paint in red, white, tan, and green (I used Napa Red, Antique White, Light Mocha, White Wash, and Pine Green by DecoArt)
* 1-step crackle medium (I used Weathered Wood by DecoArt)
* white or ivory votive candle or tea light
* scissors
* 1" foam paintbrush
* 1" scruffy old paintbrush
* medium-grit sandpaper
* Gem-Tac Glue
* plastic plate or palette
* power drill with ¼" drill bit
* heavy-duty staple gun and staples
* iron and pressing surface

This old dresser was in poor condition, but the drawers still had potential. I gave one of the drawers a new look with an old quilt and some paint.

Directions

Paint the Drawer

1 Remove the drawer handles. Use the foam brush to basecoat red on the outside of the drawer, the fence post finials, and the flower medallions. Let all the pieces dry. (This is a distressed finish, so there is no need to sand or seal the pieces before beginning.)

2 Rub the flat side of the candle all over the painted drawer, finials, and flower medallions, focusing on the areas that would get the most natural wear. Rubbing the candle will leave a light coat of wax on the painted wood surface, which will create a resist for the top coat of paint.

3 Use a foam brush to randomly dab small areas of the drawer, finials, and flower medallions with crackle medium. Let dry according to the manufacturer's instructions.

4 On a plastic plate or palette, pour equal amounts of white, tan, and antique white paint. Lightly mix the colors together on the palette for a swirled, marbled effect, but don't blend them completely together. Apply this paint mixture to the drawer, finials, and medallions,

continuously reloading the brush with mixed colors from the palette. Let the pieces dry overnight.

5 Rub all the surfaces with medium-grit sandpaper. The paint will come off easily where the wax resist was applied, allowing the red basecoat to show through.

6 Use the foam brush to paint green on the inside of the drawer and the four wood blocks. Let the paint dry.

7 Carefully center the flower medallions on the front of the drawer and use Gem-Tac Glue to attach them. Let the glue dry.

8 Use a power drill with a ¼" drill bit to drill a hole in the center of each painted wood block (drill about 1" into the block). Turn the drawer right-side-down and drill a hole in each corner of the base for a finial. Place the finals about 1" from each side of the drawer. Insert the screw end of the finial in place to check the fit and placement

and adjust if needed. To finish, thread a 2" wood block onto each exposed screw on the inside of the drawer, covering the screw completely and securing the leg in place.

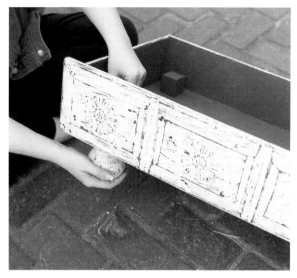

Make the Quilt-Covered Lid

Note: Many home improvement stores will cut the wood to your measurements.

1 Measure the drawer opening. Cut (or have cut) ½" thick plywood to fit the top. Double check the fit before proceeding. The plywood should be too large to fit inside the drawer, but not so large that it overhangs the edges. Cut the 4" thick upholstery foam the same size as the plywood.

2 Lay the plywood piece on your work surface. Position the upholstery foam piece on top and use Gem-Tac Glue to secure it in place. Let the glue dry.

3 Iron the quilt to remove any wrinkles. Place the quilt face down on your work surface. Carefully center the plywood/foam piece foam-side-down on top of the quilt. Wrap the quilt around the foam and place it on top of the ottoman to make sure the design is centered. When you are happy with the layout, use scissors to trim the quilt around the plywood/foam piece, leaving 8" of quilt fabric on each side.

4 Starting on one long side, pull the quilt over the edge of the wood and staple it in place. Starting from the center, work your way to each corner, pulling the quilt taut as you work. Repeat for the other long side, pulling the quilt firmly as you work so it will lay flat on top of the foam.

5 Working on a short side, fold the fabric "gift wrap" style and staple it in place. Repeat for the other short side.

6 Cut a piece of vintage sheet fabric 2" smaller on all sides than the fabric-covered lid. Fold the edges under 1" on all sides and press. Carefully center the sheet in place on the underside of the fabric-covered ottoman lid, covering all the staples, and glue it in place. Let the glue dry.

7 Place the fabric-covered lid on top of the ottoman, aligning the edges of the lid with the edges of the drawer. Because the lid is removable, you can still use the drawer for storage. However, this piece is not sturdy enough to sit on.

This ottoman is a lovely addition to any room, but is not strong enough to be used as seating.

Scottie-Shaped Pillow

This cute Scottie pillow is made from a single pattern piece and whips up in no time. Make one Scottie as a charming accent for any room, or pile a bunch of Scotties made from different fabrics in a painted pail or basket.

Directions

Note: This project uses a ¼" seam allowance.

1 Make the plastic template: Use a pencil to trace the Scottie pattern from page 127 onto the clear plastic template sheet. Cut out the template.

2 Cut two Scotties: Place a cutter quilt scrap on a flat work surface with the right side up. Place the plastic template on top of the scrap. Move the template around until you are happy with the way the cut piece will look. (Experiment with different areas of the quilt until you find one you like.) Trace around the Scottie template with a water-soluble fabric marker. Repeat, for a total of two Scotties.

3 Place the body pieces with right sides together and sew all the way around, leaving a 3" opening for turning. Turn the body right side out and press. Stuff firmly with fiberfill and hand stitch the opening closed.

4 Wrap the black grosgrain ribbon around the neck and tie a bow. Use two strands of black embroidery floss to stitch the gold bell charm to the ribbon at the base of the neck.

5 Use scissors to snip the shanks from the black buttons. Glue a black button eye to each side of the face, referring to the photo for placement.

6 Use the black embroidery floss to add a triangle nose and a mouth to the face, if desired.

You will need:

Vintage linens
* 2 cutter quilt scraps, at least 8" x 10" each

Other fabrics and trims
* 14" length of black grosgrain ribbon, ⅝" wide
* 2 round shank style black buttons, ¼" diameter
* gold heart charm, ⅜" tall
* black embroidery floss

Other supplies
* scissors
* clear plastic template sheet
* pencil
* water-soluble fabric marker
* fiberfill
* needle and thread
* hot glue gun and glue sticks
* sewing machine and accessories (this project can be done by hand, but it will be more time-consuming)

This Scottie is made from white chenille instead of a quilt piece. I used a gold bell charm to accent the collar.

Chenille Baby Quilt

Soft, cuddly vintage chenille combines with vintage and reproduction cotton fabrics for this cute baby quilt. The quilt is fast and easy to make – just cut, sew, and wash for an instant snuggly cover for your favorite baby.

You will need:

Vintage linens
* ivory chenille twin size bedspread
* total 1½ yards from assorted scraps of vintage and reproduction fabrics in the following colors: pink, blue, green, purple, yellow (I used baby dresses, aprons, vintage baby blankets, pajama pants, and other garment scraps)
* total 1½ yards from assorted scraps of white and off-white fabrics (I used vintage sheets and pillowcases)

Other supplies
* fabric basting spray
* cardboard or foam core scrap, at least 12" x 12"
* rotary cutter, ruler, and mat, or ruler, fabric marker, and scissors
* sewing machine and accessories
* iron and pressing surface

Directions

Note: This project uses a ½" seam allowance.

1 Cut all the fabrics into 5" x 5" squares. Try stacking the cotton fabrics to cut as many as 10 at a time. Use a rotary cutter, ruler, and mat to cut the fabrics as listed below:

From the vintage and reproduction prints cut:
(20) 5" pink squares
(16) 5" blue squares
(20) 5" green squares
(12) 5" yellow squares
(4) 5" purple squares

From the white prints cut:
(72) 5" squares

From the chenille cut:
(144) 5" squares
Note: *Depending on the thickness of the chenille, you may find it easier to mark the squares with a fabric marking pen, then cut with scissors. Very thick chenille can be difficult to cut accurately with a rotary cutter.*

2 Baste the squares: Working in a well-ventilated area, use a piece of scrap cardboard or foam core as a work surface. Lay four to six pieces of chenille (depending on the size of your work surface) fluffy-side-down on your work surface. Spray each chenille square with a light, even amount of basting spray.

Because the fabric didn't show up well on foam core, it's shown on a dark cutting board surface.

Top each chenille square with a right-side-up vintage or reproduction fabric, lining up the edges, and pressing the squares together. Remove the basted squares from your work surface and repeat this process until all of the vintage and reproduction fabrics are basted. Repeat, matching up the chenille and white fabrics. You will have a total of 144 basted blocks to work with.

3 Lay out the quilt: Lay the quilt out on a large flat surface such as a large table or the floor. Follow the diagram to lay out the quilt. Remember, each square is basted to another fabric – this is what gives the quilt its weight and balance. The front of the quilt is chenille squares, alternating with vintage and reproduction prints in a traditional "around the world" pattern. The back is chenille squares alternating with white and off-white fabrics. (Don't worry about the back. If you lay out the front as shown, the back will be laid out correctly as well.)

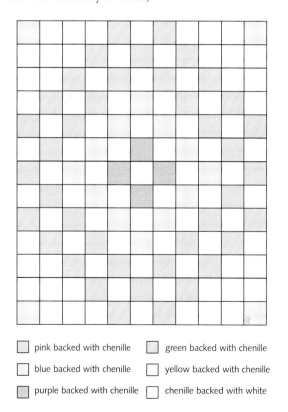

☐ pink backed with chenille   ☐ green backed with chenille

☐ blue backed with chenille   ☐ yellow backed with chenille

☐ purple backed with chenille   ☐ chenille backed with white

Starting from the center, work your way around, laying out the purple, then the blue, pink, green, yellow, and finally the blue squares. The colored squares on the diagram represent the corresponding color vintage and print fabrics. The white squares represent the chenille fabric.

4 When you are happy with the layout, begin piecing. This quilt has a ragged edge finish, which means your piecing doesn't have to be as perfect as on a traditional quilt. If your squares are a little off when you finish the assembly, it won't affect the look of the finished project.

Start with the top row and sew the pieces together in order. Be sure to sew the quilt so the raw edges will be on top (the side with the colored squares). Always place the wrong sides together as you work. Once the row is sewn, place it back on your layout surface so you can keep the pieces in order. Repeat for each row.

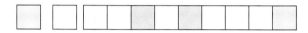

After you have sewn all the individual squares into rows, stitch the rows together. Remember to stitch so the raw edges will be on top, placing the wrong sides together.

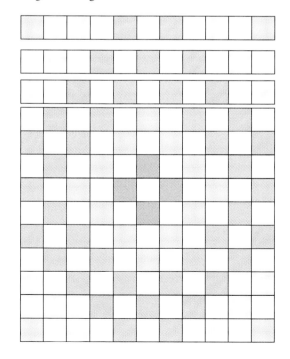

5 Snip the seam allowances: Use scissors to snip all the seam allowances. Make a cut almost to the stitching line along each seam on the face of the quilt. Snip the quilt every ½", taking special care not to snip past the sewing line.

6 Wash and dry the quilt: This quilt is not complete until you wash and dry it, which will give it a fluffy appearance. Place it in the washer and run it through a normal cycle with detergent and fabric softener. Don't be alarmed when you remove the quilt from the washer – it will look pretty raggedy! Dry it in the dryer and remove it promptly for a soft, cuddly quilt ready for baby.

Special Occasion
Chair Cover

Give a fast facelift to a plain wood or metal chair of any size with this simple sheet slipcover. Use the finished chair for a tea party, bridal or baby shower, or other special event.

Directions

1 Drape the chair: Drape the sheet over the chair, covering the chair completely. The sheet should just touch the floor in the front, and the excess fabric should hang over the back. If your sheet has a decorative edge, put the decorative edge at the back of the chair.

2 Use your fingers to gather the sheet at the back of the chair and pin the gathers in place.

3 Make the bow: Tear an 18" wide strip from the coordinating sheet. To do this, snip the fabric with the scissors to mark the 18", then tear a strip the length of the sheet. The sheet should tear easily and in a straight line. Fold the strip in half lengthwise with the right sides together and stitch ½" from the torn edge. Turn and press, positioning the tube of fabric so

You will need:

Vintage linens
* pretty vintage flat sheet for the cover, twin size or larger
* coordinating flat sheet for the bow, twin size or larger

Other supplies
* wood chair (or metal folding chair)
* 3 safety pins, 1"
* scissors
* ruler
* needle and thread to match the sheet
* sewing machine and accessories
* iron and pressing surface

the seam is in the center.

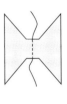

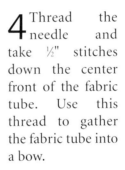

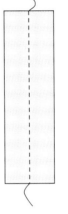

4 Thread the needle and take ½" stitches down the center front of the fabric tube. Use this thread to gather the fabric tube into a bow.

5 Tear a 6" wide strip of fabric from the sheet. Tie the fabric strip around the bow and let the ends hang free. Tear a 2" wide strip of fabric from the sheet. Tie the strip around the tails of the bow and knot to secure. Pin the bow in place on the back of the chair, using one safety pin for each side of the bow.

Garden Tea Party

Create a special outdoor setting for tea for two. All the linens used here are washable, so don't worry about spills or staining. Refer to the directions on page 72 to cover two chairs with pink vintage sheets, then follow the directions below for the table covering. Use your prettiest pink and white dishes and add some deep pink roses to complete the look.

Refer to the directions on page 72

You will need:

Vintage linens
* white vintage sheet for the bottom table cover, twin size or larger
* pink flat sheet for the top table cover, twin size or larger
* white crocheted table topper, 24" x 24"

Other supplies
* table with rectangle or square top
* measuring tape
* needle and thread to match the sheet
* scissors
* water-soluble fabric marker
* sewing machine and accessories
* iron and pressing surface

Directions

1 Drape the table: Drape the white sheet over the table, covering it completely. Let any excess fabric pile on the floor at the base of the table.

2 Measure the tabletop and add 24" to the length and 24" to the width of the tabletop. Mark and cut the pink sheet to this size. Turn under the sheet edges 1" on all sides, press, and stitch to hem.

3 Place the pink cover on the tabletop, centering it carefully. At the center front of the table, use the needle and thread to gather the fabric 6" from the edge. Knot the thread to secure. Repeat for the sides and back.

4 Place the crocheted table topper diagonally on top of the table, allowing the corners to hang over the edges as shown. Set the table as desired. The table in the photo is set with vintage pink and gold china and white Fire King teacups, saucers, and berry bowls

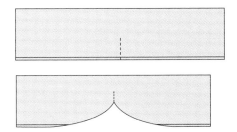

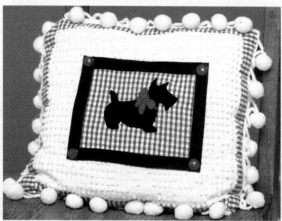

Chapter 4

Vintage Clothing Projects

The projects featured in this chapter are made from vintage clothing items. Some also feature photographs. Make these items from favorite garments, or as mementos of a loved one.

Blue Jeans Tote

Recycle a pair of old jeans into a fashionable tote bag. Use the pockets to hold your keys, glasses, and cell phone. I used a pair of size 10 women's jeans, but other sizes can be substituted as needed. If you don't have an old pair of jeans to cut up, check a thrift or charity shop – you can usually find a huge selection of jeans for around $1 a pair.

Directions

Note: *This project uses a ½" seam allowance and is assembled so that the seam allowances are on the outside.*

1 Cut the fabrics: Cut the legs off the jeans. Use scissors to cut up the inseam of one leg, opening it up. Repeat for the other leg. Use the leg fabric for the bottom, sides, and handle of the bag.

From the jeans cut:
2" x 16" strip for the bag bottom
3" x 30" strip for the bag handle
Note: *Depending on the length of your jeans, you may need to piece the handle strip.*
(2) 12" x 16" rectangles from the top of the jeans. Include one front pocket and one back pocket in each rectangle. Discard the zipper and back seam.
(2) 2" x 12" strips for the bag sides

From the pink sheet cut:
2" x 16" strip for the bag bottom
3" x 30" strip for the bag handle
(2) 12" x 16" rectangles
(2) 2" x 12" strips for the bag sides

You will need:

Vintage linens
* pair denim jeans, any adult size
* ladies embroidered hankie, any size
* pink cotton sheet, any size

Other supplies
* scissors
* water-soluble fabric marker
* ruler
* fabric basting spray
* needle and thread
* scrap piece of foam core or cardboard
* sewing machine and accessories (this project can be done by hand, but it will be more time-consuming)
* iron and pressing surface

2 Baste the pieces: Working in a well ventilated area, use a piece of scrap cardboard or foam core as a work surface. Lay a 12" x 16" denim rectangle on your work surface with the right side down. Spray with a light, even coat of basting spray. Top with a right-side-up 12" x 16" pink rectangle, lining up the edges and pressing the pieces together with an iron. Remove the pieces from your work surface and repeat this process until all the denim and pink fabrics are paired up and basted.

3 Keep the basted pairs together as you work. With the pink sides together, stitch a 2" x 12" piece to each side of a 12" x 16" rectangle. Stitch the remaining 12" x 16" rectangle to one of the side pieces. Press.

16"		16"	
12"			12"
2"		2"	

4 Stitch the remaining side of the 12" x 16" rectangle to the remaining side piece, forming a fabric tube. This will be the body of the bag.

5 Stitch the 2" x 16" strip to the bottom of the tube. Stitch around all the sides.

6 Stitch around the 3" x 30" handle pieces. Stitch the ends of the handle in place at each side of the tote bag.

7 Use scissors to snip the seam allowances all around the tote bag and handle. Cut every ½" up to, but not through the stitching. Wash and dry the tote bag.

8 Decide which side of the bag will be the front and tuck the embroidered handkerchief in the pocket.

Daddy's Suits Teddy

This teddy bear was made with pieces from several men's suit jackets. Make him as shown or use men's flannel or dress shirts instead of suits.

You will need:

Vintage linens
* fabrics from men's clothing, ½ yard total from suit jackets, vests, shirts, ties, etc.

Trims
* ½ yard of black grosgrain ribbon, ¼" wide

Other supplies
* scissors
* pencil
* clear plastic template sheet
* water-soluble fabric marker
* fiberfill
* long tapestry needle and quilter's thread to match the fabric
* sewing machine and accessories (this project can be done by hand, but it will be more time-consuming)
* iron and pressing surface

Directions

Note: This project uses a ¼" seam allowance.

1 Make the pattern templates: Use a pencil to trace the Bear pattern pieces from pages 124-126 onto the clear plastic template sheet. Cut out each template.

2 Cut out the pattern pieces: Place the templates on top of the fabric. Trace around each template with the water-soluble marker. For identical, easy-to-sew pieces, lay two pieces of fabric with the right sides together, transfer the pattern to the top piece, and cut out both pieces at the same time. These pieces will match exactly and be in the right position for sewing. Use this technique for the legs, arms, ears, and body.

3 Make the arms: Place two arm pieces with right sides together and sew all the way around, leaving an opening for turning. Turn right side out and press. Stuff firmly with fiberfill and hand stitch the opening closed. Repeat for the second arm.

4 Make the legs and feet: Place two leg pieces with right sides together. Stitch around the sides and top of the leg, leaving an opening at the side for turning. Leave the bottom of the leg open to attach the footpad. Place a footpad on the opening with the right side facing in. Carefully hand stitch around the foot. After the footpad is stitched in place, turn the leg right side out and press. Stuff firmly and hand stitch the opening closed. Repeat for the second leg.

5 Make the ears: Place two ear pieces with right sides together. Stitch around the sides and top of the ear, leaving the base open for turning. Turn right side out and press. Stuff loosely and hand stitch the opening closed. Repeat for the second ear.

6 Make the body: Place two body pieces with right sides together. Stitch around the sides and bottom of the body, leaving the top open for turning and head attachment. Turn the body right side out and press. Stuff firmly.

7 Make the head: Place a side head piece on the center head piece with right sides together. Stitch around the sides and back of the head A to B on the pattern, leaving the bottom open for turning and attachment. With right sides together, stitch the remaining side head piece to the other side of the center head piece. Turn the head right side out and press. Stuff firmly.

Assemble the Bear

1 Use the photo as a guide to assemble the bear using a long tapestry needle and quilter's thread.

2 Place the head on top of the body. Match up the front of the face with the front of the body (the curved "tummy" of the bear goes in the front). Hand stitch the head and body

together, easing the fabric if needed. This attachment does not have to be perfect – it will be covered up by ribbon in a later step.

3 Stitch an ear to each side of the head, allowing them to touch in the center.

4 Attach an arm to each side of the body just below the neck by bringing the needle in through the back of the body and out the side, passing through the top of the arm. Take a stitch, bringing the needle back through the arm and out the back of the body. Stitch again for a firm attachment. Repeat for the second arm.

5 Attach a leg to each side of the body just above the bottom by bringing the needle in through the back of the body and out the side, passing through the top of the leg. Take a stitch, bringing the needle back through the leg and out the back of the body. Stitch again for a firm attachment. Repeat for the second leg.

6 Add the buttons: Use Gem-Tac Glue to attach the ½" black buttons to cover the attachment points on the arms and legs. Glue the round black buttons to the face for the eyes and the oval button for the nose. Experiment with the placement of the facial buttons – different positions will result in different facial expressions. When you are happy with the bear's expression, glue the buttons in place.

7 Tie the grosgrain ribbon around the neck and trim the ribbon ends as desired.

Prom Dress Bunny

The fabric used for this bunny came from a pink 1950s prom dress. Prom and bridesmaid dresses are easy to find at used clothing stores or garage sales.

Directions

Note: This project uses a ¼" seam allowance.

1 Make the plastic templates: Use a pencil to trace the Bunny pattern pieces from pages 124-126 onto the clear plastic template sheet. Cut out each template.

2 Cut out the pattern pieces: Place the templates on top of the fabric. Trace around each template with the water-soluble marker. For identical, easy-to-sew pieces, lay two pieces of fabric with the right sides together, transfer the pattern to the top piece, and cut out both pieces at the same time. These pieces will match exactly and be in the right position for sewing. Use this technique for the legs, arms, ears, and body. Cut two ear pieces and two arm pieces from the ivory fabric, and the rest of the pieces from the pink fabric.

3 Make the arms: Place one ivory and one pink arm piece with right sides together and sew all the way around, leaving an opening for turning. Turn the arm right side out and press. Stuff firmly with fiberfill and hand stitch the opening closed. Repeat for the second arm.

4 Make the legs and feet: Place two leg pieces with right sides together. Stitch around the sides and top of the leg, leaving an opening at the side for turning. Leave the bottom of the leg open to attach the footpad. Place a footpad on the opening with the right side facing in. Carefully hand stitch around the foot. Once the footpad is stitched in place, turn the leg right side out and press. Stuff firmly and hand stitch the opening closed. Repeat for the second leg.

5 Make the ears: Place one ivory and one pink ear piece with right sides together. Stitch around the sides and top of the ear, leaving the base open for turning. Turn the ear right side out and press. Hand stitch the opening closed. Repeat for the second ear.

6 Make the body: Place two body pieces with right sides together. Stitch around the sides and bottom of the body, leaving the top open for turning and for attaching the head. Turn the body right side out and press. Stuff firmly.

7 Make the head: Place a side head piece against the center head piece with the right sides together. Stitch around the sides and back of head A to B on the pattern, leaving the bottom open for turning and attachment. With right sides together, stitch the remaining side head piece to the other side of the center head piece. Turn the head right side out and press. Stuff firmly.

You will need:

Vintage linens
* fabric from pink women's formal dress, about ¼ yard total
* small ivory scrap, at least 8" x 8"

Trims
* ½ yard of grosgrain ribbon to match the fabric, ¼" wide
* 4 round pink buttons, ¼" diameter
* 2 round pearl buttons, ⅜" diameter
* oval pearl button, ½" wide

Other supplies
* scissors
* pencil
* clear plastic template sheet
* water-soluble fabric marker
* fiberfill
* Gem-Tac Glue
* long tapestry needle and quilter's thread to match the fabric
* sewing machine and accessories (this project can be done by hand, but it will be more time-consuming)
* iron and pressing surface

Assemble the Bunny

1 Use the photo as a guide to assemble the bunny using a long tapestry needle and quilter's thread.

2 Place the head on top of the body. Match up the front of the face with the front of the body (the curved "tummy" goes in front). Hand stitch the head and body together, easing the fabric if needed. This attachment does not have to be perfect – it will be covered by ribbon in a later step.

3 Stitch an ear to each side of the head.

4 Attach an arm to each side of the body just below the neck by bringing the needle in through the back of the body and out the side, passing through the top of the arm. Take a stitch, bringing the needle back through the arm and out the back of the body. Repeat for a firm attachment.

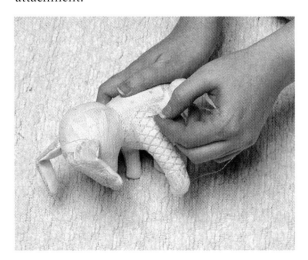

5 Attach a leg to each side of the body just above the bunny's seat by bringing the needle in through the back of the body and out the side, passing through the top of the leg. Take a stitch, bringing the needle back through the leg and out the back of the body. Repeat for a firm attachment.

6 Add the buttons: Use Gem-Tac Glue to attach the pink buttons to cover the attachment points on the arms and legs. Glue the round pearl buttons to the face for the eyes and the oval button for the nose. Experiment with the placement of the facial buttons – different positions will create different facial expressions. When you are happy with the bunny's expression, glue the buttons in place.

7 Tie the grosgrain ribbon around the neck and trim the ribbon ends as desired.

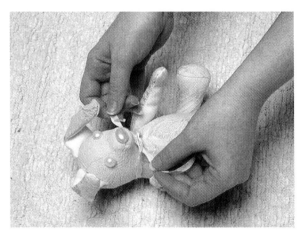

Appliqué
Scottie Pillow

This perky little Scottie dog is the perfect companion for crisp
red gingham and fluffy white chenille. I snipped the gingham from a
vintage apron and rescued the pom-pom fringe from an absolutely
terrible set of 1970s curtains.

You will need:

Vintage linens
* large white chenille scrap, at least 24" x 24"
* red and white gingham clothing scrap, ¼ yard (new red gingham can be substituted)
* scrap of solid black cotton, at least 4" x 4"
* scrap of solid red cotton, at least 2" x 2"

Trims
* 1½ yards of white pom-pom trim
* 1 yard of black grosgrain ribbon, ½" wide
* 4 red glass buttons, 3/8" diameter (I used vintage buttons)
* large scrap of fusible webbing, at least 10" x 10"

Other supplies
* rotary cutter, ruler, and mat, or ruler, fabric marker, and scissors
* clear plastic template sheet
* pencil
* fiberfill
* needle and thread
* embroidery floss in black and red
* Fabri-Tac Glue
* 1" foam brush
* sewing machine and accessories (this project can be done by hand, but it will be more time-consuming)
* iron and pressing surface

Directions

Note: *This project uses a ¼" seam allowance.*

1 Cut the fabrics.

From the white chenille fabric cut:
10" x 11" rectangle for pillow front
12" x 13" rectangle for pillow back

From the red gingham fabric cut:
5" x 6" rectangle
(2) 11" x 1¼" strips
(2) 12" x 1¼" strips

From the fusible webbing cut:
4" x 4" square
2" x 2" square

2 Make plastic templates: Use a pencil to trace the Appliqué Scottie and the Bow patterns from page 126 onto the clear plastic template sheet and cut them out.

3 Place the 4" x 4" black fabric scrap right-side-down on your pressing surface. Top it with the 4" x 4" square of fusible webbing, adhesive-side-down. Follow the manufacturer's directions to fuse the pieces.
Note: *Fusible webbing has two sides – a webby, textured adhesive side, and a smooth paper backing. Make sure you place the webbing adhesive-side-down before touching it with an iron!*

4 Place the 2" x 2" red fabric scrap right-side-down on your pressing surface. Top it with the 2" x 2" square of fusible webbing, adhesive-side-down. Follow the manufacturer's directions to fuse the pieces.

5 Place the black fabric scrap right-side-down on your work surface (the paper backing of the fusible webbing should be facing up). Place the plastic Scottie template on top of the paper backing and trace around the template with a pencil. Cut it out on the marked line.

6 Place the red fabric scrap right-side-down on your work surface (the paper backing of the fusible webbing should be facing up). Place the plastic bow template on top of the paper backing and trace around the template with a pencil. Cut it out on the marked line.

7 Place the 5" x 6" red gingham rectangle right-side-up on your pressing surface. Peel the paper backing from the Scottie and center him in place on the rectangle. Be sure to place the Scottie with the right (fabric) side up, and the adhesive side down. Follow the manufacturer's directions to iron the Scottie in place.

8 Peel the paper backing from the bow and center it on the Scottie's neck. Follow the manufacturer's directions to iron the bow in place.

9 Cover the raw edges by hand stitching around the Scottie and the bow using two strands of embroidery floss. Use black floss for the Scottie and red floss for the bow.

10 Add the gingham border: Place the 10" x 11" chenille rectangle right-side-up on a flat work surface. Place a 1¼" x 11" red gingham strip at the top and at the bottom. Stitch in place, keeping the right sides together and lining up the edges as you work. Press.

11 Place a 1¼" x 12" red ging-ham strip at each side of the chenille piece. Stitch in place, keeping the right sides together and lining up the edges as you work. Press.

gingham borders

white chenille

12 Carefully center the appliquéd rectangle of red gingham on the white chenille and stitch it in place. There is no need to finish the edges, as they will be covered with grosgrain ribbon.

white chenille

Scottie appliqué

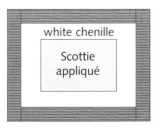

13 Use fabric glue to attach strips of gros-grain ribbon around the red gingham. (You can sew these in place if you prefer.) Let the glue dry completely before proceeding.

14 Place the completed pillow front right-side-up on your work surface. Place the pom-pom fringe on top of the pillow front, matching up the raw edges. The pom-poms should face the center of the pillow. Stitch in place.

Assemble the Pillow

1 Place the pillow front and chenille back with the right sides together, lining up the edges. Stitch around the edges of the pillow, leaving an opening for turning and stuffing.

2 Turn and press. Stuff firmly with fiberfill and hand stitch the opening closed.

3 Use a hot glue gun to glue a red button in place on top of the ribbon in each corner.

Family Memories Pillow

Make a unique accent pillow featuring a photo of your family. I made this pillow using a black and white photo of my husband's family (he's the cutie in the front!), but you can substitute a color photo if you prefer.

Directions

Note: This project uses a ¼" seam allowance.

1 Transfer the family photo to the 9" x 9" piece of white fabric, centering it carefully. Use one of the photo transfer methods described in Crafting Techniques, pages 115 and 116. After the image is transferred to the fabric, avoid placing the iron directly on the image.

2 Use the rotary cutter to trim around the photo, leaving a 1" fabric border around all sides of the photo.

3 Cut two 1" x 9" and two 1" x 7" strips of the ivory silk fabric. With the right sides together, sew a 1" x 7" strip to each side of the photo.

Press the seam open without touching the iron to the fabric photo. Trim the edges if needed. Repeat with the 1" x 9" strips on the top and bottom of the photo.

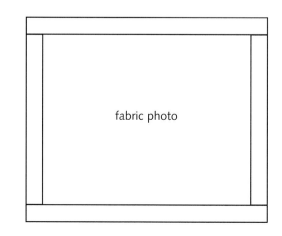

4 Cut a 9" x 11" rectangle of pink print cotton. Center the fabric photo piece on the pink fabric, with both right sides up, and stitch around the edges to secure.

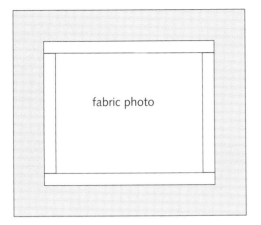

5 Make a lace border: Cut two 9" and two 7" strips of the gathered ivory lace. With the right side up, topstitch a 7" strip of lace to each side edge of the ivory. Place the lace right on the edge of the ivory silk and zigzag stitch over both pieces. Trim the lace edge as needed. Repeat with the 9" strips of lace on the top and bottom.

6 Cut four 2" x 11" strips of ivory and pink striped fabric. With right sides together, stitch a piece of striped fabric to the top and bottom of the pink print rectangle. Press the seam and trim as needed. Repeat for each side.

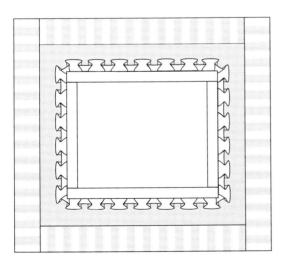

You will need:

Vintage linens
* fabric from women's or girl's clothing, as listed below:
¼ yard of pink print cotton
¼ yard of ivory and pink striped cotton
½ yard of heavyweight ivory silk fabric
  (I used fabric from a vintage wedding gown)

Other fabrics and trims
* 4 pink glass shank buttons, ½" diameter
* large scrap of white cotton, cut 9" x 9"
* 1 yard of gathered ivory lace, 1" wide
* 24" of flat pink satin ribbon, ½" wide
* 24" of ivory fringe, 2½" wide

Other supplies
* family photo, 5" x 7"
* photo transfer materials (see Crafting Techniques, pages 115 and 116)
* rotary cutter and mat, or ruler, fabric marker, and scissors
* fiberfill
* needle and ivory thread
* sewing machine and accessories (this project can be done by hand, but it will be more time-consuming)
* iron and pressing surface

7 Cut two 3" x 11" rectangles of ivory silk. With right sides together, stitch an ivory silk rectangle to each side of the pillow front. Press the seams and trim as needed.

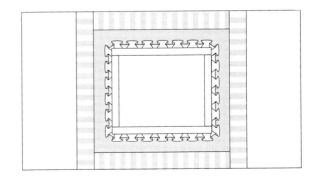

8 Cut two 12" strips of pink satin ribbon. Using the photo as a guide, lay one strip along the seam of the ivory silk rectangle with the right side up. Stitch in place. Repeat for the other side. Hand stitch a ½" pink button to each corner of the fabric photo.

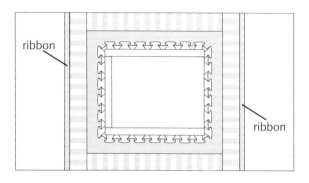

9 Use the rotary cutter and mat to cut a pillow back from the ivory silk. Cut a piece the same size as the pillow front. With right sides together, pin the pillow back to the pillow front.

10 Cut two 12" strips of ivory fringe, one for each side. Insert the fringe between the pillow layers on each side, with the fringes facing toward the pillow center. Stitch around the edge of the pillow, leaving a 4" opening on one side for turning and stuffing.

11 Trim the corners and turn the pillow right side out through the opening. Press.

12 Stuff the pillow with fiberfill to the desired firmness and hand stitch the opening closed.

Family Memories Shadowbox

This box is a unique way to show off a special family photo. The three-dimensional shape of the box allows you to display some accent pieces along with the photo. Use bits of lace made by an ancestor, an old hankie, or special piece of costume jewelry as embellishments.

You will need:

Vintage linens
* small vintage textile (hankie, collar, cuff, or napkin with a pretty lace edge)
* ivory crocheted doily, 5"

Other fabrics and trims
* 2 white rose buttons, ½" diameter
* 12" of plastic ivory string pearls, ⅛" wide
* flat-backed oval plastic pearl medallion, ¾" tall

Other supplies
* 7" x 7" wood shadowbox frame (a small drawer can be substituted)
* family photo
* 1 crystal globe drawer pull, 1" diameter
* acrylic craft paint in white, taupe, russet, and gold (I used White Wash, Taupe, Metallic Russet, and Glorious Gold Americanas by DecoArt)
* 1-step crackle medium (I used Weathered Wood by DecoArt)
* sheet of scrapbook paper with written text, or a color copy of an old letter
* sheet of white cardstock
* pencil
* decorative-edge scissors
* thick white craft glue, or glue gun and glue sticks
* votive candle or tea light, any color
* matches
* drill with ¼" drill bit
* 1" foam brush
* ½" or 1" flat paintbrush
* old scruffy paintbrush
* paper towels

Directions

Prepare the Shadowbox

1 Use the foam brush to paint the inside and outside of the shadowbox with white. Let the paint dry. (There is no need to sand or seal the shadowbox before beginning.)

2 Use the foam brush to apply crackle medium to the shadowbox. Let it dry.

3 Use the flat paintbrush to top the crackle medium with a thin wash of taupe (mix the taupe paint with an equal ratio of water). Let the paint dry.

4 Use the scruffy brush to drybrush a thin layer of gold on the outside and front of the shadowbox. Let the paint dry.

> To drybrush, load the scruffy brush with paint and brush most of the paint on a paper towel or piece of scrap paper. Whisk the dry brush lightly over the project surface, allowing the paint to color the raised surfaces and edges.

5 Use the power drill to drill a ¼" hole in the top of the shadowbox, centering the hole carefully.

Prepare the Box Interior

1 If desired, make a color photocopy of your family photograph (a color copy might be better if you only have one original!). If you have multiple copies, an original photo will work for this project.

2 Use decorative-edge scissors to trim the edges of the photo. Use a thin application of thick white craft glue to attach the photo to the white cardstock. Let the glue dry.

3 Use scissors to cut a liner for the box from the letter or written text scrapbook paper. Trace the outline of the shadowbox on the scrapbook paper and cut it out.

4 Light the candle and burn all the edges of the lining paper and the white cardstock. This step is best done over a sink, and you should burn only a small area at a time, blowing out the flame as you go. Use care when burning or working with a lit candle!

Note: For this step, you do not want a roaring flame, just enough to burn the edges and make them "crinkle" up. Practice on a piece of scrap paper.

5 Use the foam brush and thick white craft glue to attach the box liner and photograph to the inside of the box, referring to the photo for placement. Let the glue dry.

Add the Embellishments

1 Use thick white craft glue to attach a ¾" white rose button to the upper left and lower right corners of the liner paper. Let the glue dry.

2 Use russet paint to age the plastic string pearls and pearl medallion. Brush the russet paint on with a foam brush, then wipe the paint away with a paper towel, allowing the paint to settle in the crevices and between the pearls. Let the paint dry.

3 Roll the piece of vintage textile into a loose cone. The finished size should be about 4" long. I used a piece of a vintage dress collar. Wrap the painted string pearls around the middle of the vintage textile piece and place it inside the shadowbox. Adjust for fit, allowing a loop of pearls to rest on the base of the box. When you are happy with the look of these pieces, glue them in place.

4 Top with the painted pearl medallion glued in place, referring to the photo for placement. Let the glue dry.

5 Insert the screw for the drawer pull in the drilled hole at the top of the shadowbox. Sandwich the crocheted doily between the top of the shadowbox and the drawer pull to secure.

Dad's Memories Quilt

Use candid family photos and fabric from dad's suits, ties, and casual clothing to make this handsome memory quilt. The log-cabin-style blocks work up quickly, and the uniform size of the photo blocks makes assembly a snap. Piece the fabrics randomly for best results.

You will need:

Vintage linens
* fabric from men's garments, 3 yards total (I used fabric from three suit jackets, 14 ties, one pair of jeans, and small scraps from other garments)

Other fabrics and trims
* 20 buttons snipped from men's garments, in assorted materials and sizes
* 1 yard of white cotton, 44" wide for the photo blocks
* 1 yard of burgundy cotton for the border
* ½ yard of charcoal gray cotton for the binding

* 2 yards of unbleached muslin, 90" wide for the quilt back

Other supplies
* 30 family photos, 5" x 5" or smaller (resize your photos as needed on a computer or photocopier)
* photo transfer materials (see Crafting Techniques, pages 115 and 116)
* cotton quilt batting, twin mattress size
* rotary cutter and mat
* needle and thread
* sewing machine and accessories
* iron and pressing surface

Directions

Note: This project uses a ¼" seam allowance.

1 Cut 30 6" x 6" blocks from the white fabric.

2 Carefully center the family photos on the white blocks and transfer them to the fabric using one of the photo transfer methods described in Crafting Techniques on pages 115 and 116. After the images are transferred to the fabric, avoid placing the iron directly on them.

3 From the men's garments, cut 240 strips 2" wide x 10" long for piecing.

4 Piece the blocks: Use a fabric photo square as the center of each log-cabin-style block. The blocks are pieced by adding fabric borders one strip at a time and trimming as you work. Select a fabric photo square. With right sides together, place a fabric strip at the right side of the square, lining up the edges. Stitch in place, press, and trim. Use the same technique to add a fabric strip to the bottom, other side, and top.

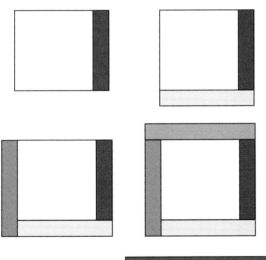

5 Use the same technique to add a second set of fabric border strips around the block. Repeat until you've completed a total of 30 blocks.

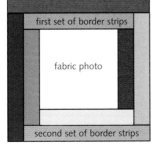

6 Use the rotary cutter and mat to square the completed blocks.

7 Arrange the completed blocks on the floor in six rows of five blocks each. Rearrange the blocks around until you are happy with the composition. Sew the blocks into rows.

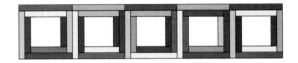

8 Stitch the rows together to finish the quilt top.

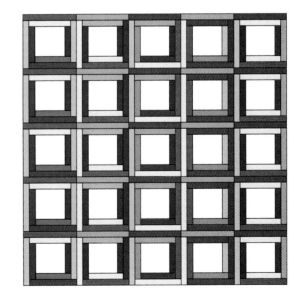

9 Add the border: From the burgundy cotton, cut eight 4" x 44" strips. With the right sides together, stitch two burgundy pieces together to form a 4" x 88" strip. Repeat for the remaining strips. With the right sides together, stitch a border strip to each side of the quilt top. Press and trim as needed. Repeat at the top and the bottom of the quilt top.

10 Layer the right-side-down quilt back, batting, and right-side-up quilt top. Baste with fabric basting spray and quilt as desired. You can quilt by hand or machine, or have the piece professionally quilted.

Note: Professional quilting is a surprisingly afford-able option and worth considering if you enjoy design and piecing more than quilting. Mine was quilted by Pat Roman of the Island Threads Quilt Shop with a meander pattern using variegated green and beige thread.

The quilting is complete but you need to add a few buttons and bind the edges.

11 Bind the edges using the charcoal cotton fabric. Cut and piece 3" strips of charcoal fabric to bind your quilt. For each side of the quilt, place a binding strip right-side-down on the face of the quilt. Stitch it in place and press.

Fold the free edge of the binding strip under ¼" and press. Fold the binding to the back of the quilt and hand stitch it in place.

Note: Refer to a basic quilting book for in-depth directions for binding your quilt.

12 Hand stitch a button at the corners of each of the center blocks.

Vintage buttons add a special touch.

The memory quilt makes a meaningful and attractive wall piece.

Mom's Memories Quilt

Use family photos of all sizes to make this scrapbook-style quilt. The photos are pieced into uniform sized blocks, but each block layout is unique. Showcase a single large photo with a thin fabric border, or combine two, three, or four photos in a block. The embellishments are added after the quilting is complete, and any lightweight fabric item can be used.

You will need:

Vintage linens
* fabric from women's garments, 4 yards total (I used several formal dresses, some vintage cotton nightgowns, and a suit jacket)
* 2 printed handkerchiefs for piecing, any size
* ivory silk handkerchief for embellishment, any size
* white cotton lace-edged handkerchief for embellishment, any size
* ivory doily for embellishment, 13" diameter
* lace collar for embellishment, any size

Other fabrics and trims
* 1 yard of white cotton, 44" wide for the photo blocks
* 1 yard of peach cotton for the border
* ½ yard of taupe cotton for the binding

* 2 yards of unbleached muslin, 90" wide for the quilt back
* 6 gold metal charms, assorted shapes, ⅜" diameter
* buttons as desired for embellishment

Other supplies
* 20 to 25 family photos, 12" x 12" or smaller (resize photos as needed on a computer or photocopier)
* photo transfer materials (see Crafting Techniques, pages 115 and 116)
* cotton quilt batting, full mattress size
* rotary cutter and mat
* needle and thread
* sewing machine and accessories
* iron and pressing surface

Directions

Note: This project uses a ¼" seam allowance.
Note: The directions below are for the quilt shown.
Make substitutions or modify the blocks and layout
as desired.

1 Transfer the family photos to the white fabric using one of the photo transfer methods described in Crafting Techniques on pages 115 and 116. After the images have been transferred to the fabric, avoid placing the iron directly on them.

2 Use a rotary cutter and ruler to trim around the photo blocks, leaving a 1" wide border of white fabric around each photo.

3 Piece the photo blocks: Use the fabric photo piece as the center of each block. The blocks are pieced by adding fabric borders one strip at a time, and trimming as you work. Select a fabric photo square. With the right sides together, place a fabric strip at one side of the square, lining up the edges. Stitch in place, press, and trim. Use the same technique to add a fabric strip to the bottom, other side, and top. Repeat to make a total of 17 photo blocks.

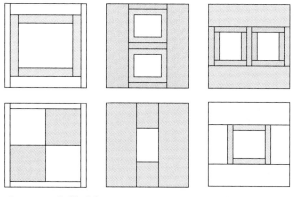

Some sample block layouts. Experiment with different widths of fabric to make different blocks. Imagine that each block is an individual scrapbook page and add photos and borders as desired. Each finished block should measure 12" x 12".

4 Make the handkerchief blocks: Measure a printed handkerchief. If needed, add borders to the top, bottom, and sides to make a 12" x 12" block. Repeat, for a total of two handkerchief blocks.

5 Make the plain blocks: Cut six 12" x 12" blocks from assorted fabrics. These blocks will be the embellishment blocks after the quilting is done.

6 Arrange the completed fabric photo, handkerchief, and embellishment blocks on the floor in five rows of five blocks each. Rearrange the blocks until you are happy with the composition. Stitch the blocks into rows, then stitch the rows together to finish the quilt top.

7 Add the border: From the peach cotton, cut eight 4" x 44" strips. With the right sides together, stitch two peach pieces together to form a 4" x 88" strip. Repeat for the remaining strips. With the right sides together, stitch a border strip to each side of the quilt top. Press and trim as needed. Repeat at the top and the bottom of the quilt top.

8 Layer the right-side-down quilt back, batting, and right-side-up quilt top. Baste with fabric basting spray and quilt as desired. You can quilt by hand or machine, or have the piece professionally quilted. Mine was professionally quilted by Pat Roman of the Island Threads Quilt Shop with a meander pattern using ivory thread.

The quilt complete with embellishments. Follow the embellishment suggestions on page 99, or use your own vintage pieces to add a special touch to Mom's quilt.

9 Bind the edges using the taupe cotton fabric. Cut and piece 3" strips of taupe fabric to bind your quilt. For each side of the quilt, place a binding strip right-side-down on the face of the quilt. Stitch it in place and press. Fold the free edge of the binding strip under ¼" and press. Fold the binding to the back of the quilt and hand stitch it in place.

Note: *Refer to a basic quilting book for in-depth directions for binding your quilt.*

Add the Embellishments

1 Hand stitch the star doily to one of the embellishment blocks. Stitch a button to the center of the doily and add a gold charm to each "arm."

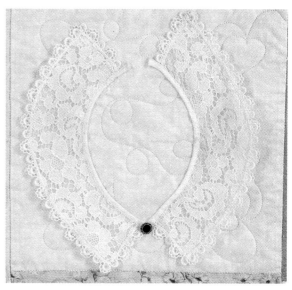

Hand stitch a vintage lace collar to your quilt for an easy, feminine touch.

Use pretty buttons and charms to add a bit of sparkle to your quilt.

2 Hand stitch the lace collar to one of the embellishment blocks. Stitch a button to the center front of the collar.

3 Fold the white lace-edged handkerchief in half diagonally. Press. Hand stitch the points of the handkerchief to one of the embellishment blocks, leaving the top open. Stitch a button to the center of the handkerchief pocket.

4 Arrange the silk handkerchief on one of the embellishment blocks. Tack it in place.

Make a plain lace-edged hankie into a pocket for tiny mementos.

This soft silk hankie drapes beautifully and adds an unexpected three-dimensional element to the otherwise flat quilt.

Scrap Projects

Use leftover pieces from your other projects or small "finds" to make these pretty, fast projects. The tassels, tote, and buttons can also be used to accent other projects.

Scrappy Tassels

Use leftover scraps from other projects to create lush tassels. Hang them from door knobs and drawer pulls, or use them to accent larger projects.

Directions

1 Use the foam brush to basecoat the outside and bottom of the candle cup with gold metallic paint. Let the paint dry. Since this is an all-over crackled finish, there is no need to sand or seal the wood pieces before painting.

2 Use the foam brush to apply crackle medium to the outside and bottom of the candle cup. Let it dry according to the manufacturer's instructions.

3 Use the scruffy paintbrush to apply a single coat of burgundy to the outside and bottom of the candle cup. Apply a thick coat of paint for large cracks or a thin coat for small cracks. Vary the direction of your brushstrokes as you apply the paint for a randomly crackled finish. The paint will crackle as it dries.

You will need:

Vintage linens
* assorted fabric scraps from men's garments

Other supplies
* wood candle cup, 1¾" tall
* acrylic craft paint in gold metallic and burgundy (I used Glorious Gold and Dark Burgundy by DecoArt)
* 1-step crackle medium (I used Weathered Wood by DecoArt)
* 24" metallic gold embroidery floss
* rotary cutter, ruler, and mat, or scissors and ruler
* scissors
* 1" foam brush
* 1" scruffy paintbrush

4 Cut the fringe strips: From the fabric scraps cut 48 strips 18" long and ¼" to ½" wide.

5 Stack the fabric strips on a flat work surface. Tie the gold metallic embroidery floss around the center of the fringe strips. Knot to secure.

6 Insert the ends of the metallic gold embroidery floss through the hole at the top of the candle cup. Draw the gold threads up through the hole, pulling the bundle of fabric strips into the cup.

7 Tie the ends of the metallic gold embroidery floss together to form a loop. Lay the completed tassel on a flat work surface and use scissors to trim the length of the fabric strips if needed.

Vary the look of your tassel by changing the fabric and paint colors. For the pink tassel, I used assorted pink fabric scraps and basecoated the candle cup with pink. After the paint dried, I used the handle end of the paintbrush to add dots of ivory. For the blue tassel, I used assorted blue and ivory fabric scraps and basecoated the candle cup with blue. After the paint dried, I applied a coat of crackle medium. After this dried, I added a coat of ivory paint.

Scrappy Tote

Use leftover pieces from larger projects for this whimsical tote. The tote shown features pink and ivory scraps, but other colors could be used.

You will need:

Vintage linens
* assorted pink and ivory scraps, ½ yard total
* 2 ivory handkerchiefs or napkins with crocheted trim
* pink pillowcase for the lining

Trim
* 4 oval pearl buttons, ¾" each

Other supplies
* ½ yard of cotton quilt batting
* fabric basting spray
* rotary cutter, ruler, and mat, or scissors and ruler
* scissors
* sewing machine and accessories
* iron and pressing surface

Directions

Note: This project uses a ¼" seam allowance.

1 Cut the fabrics.

From the pink fabric scraps cut:
6" x 7" rectangle for the pocket
(16) 3½" x 3½" squares
(2) 3" x 13" strips for the top borders
(2) 3" x 18" strips for the handles

From the ivory fabric scraps cut:
(16) 3½" x 3½" squares
(2) 3" x 18" strips for the handles

From the pillowcase cut:
(2) 12" x 15" rectangles

2 Lay out the bag front: Arrange eight pink and eight ivory 3½" squares into four rows of four blocks each, alternating the pink and ivory fabric squares.

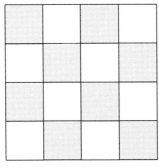

bag front

3 When you are happy with the placement of the fabrics, stitch the bag front. Start with the top row and sew the pieces together in order. After a row is sewn, place it back on your layout surface so you can keep the pieces in order. Sew all four rows.

4 Stitch the rows together.

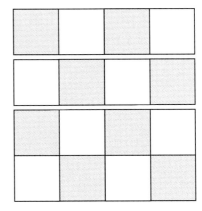

5 Repeat for the back of the bag. Press the front and back to remove any wrinkles and flatten the seams.

6 Add a pink 3" x 13" top border to the front and back pieces. Trim if needed and press.

7 Place the cotton quilt batting on a flat work surface. Spray it with a light coating of fabric basting spray and top with the bag front, right-side-up. Machine or hand quilt through both layers along the piecing lines. Repeat for the bag back.

Make the Pocket

1 Cut a 6" x 8" rectangle from an ivory handkerchief. Cut the rectangle from the edge of the handkerchief so that one side will have the crocheted trim. This will be the top of the pocket.

2 Place the 6" x 8" rectangle right-side-up on a flat work surface and top it with the 6" x 7" rectangle of pink fabric, right-side-down, lining up the bottom and side edges. Stitch around the bottom and sides, leaving the top open for turning. Turn and press.

3 Place the assembled pocket with the pink side up on a flat work surface. Fold the crocheted trim flap down over the pink fabric and press it in place.

4 Place the second ivory handkerchief on a flat work surface. Use a rotary cutter and ruler to cut one corner from the handkerchief. Cut the corner large enough to make a triangular pocket on the front of the bag. Turn the cut edge of the triangle down ½" and press. Individual handkerchief sizes vary. The finished pocket shown is 5½" x 3½". Carefully center the triangular pocket on the front of the pocket and hand stitch it in place.

5 Attach the pocket: Carefully center the pocket on the front of the bag and hand stitch it in place.

Assemble the Bag

1 Place the bag front and back with the right sides together, lining up the edges. Stitch around the sides and bottom of the bag. Turn and press the bag.

2 Place the two 12" x 13" pillowcase rectangles with right sides together, lining up the edges. Stitch around the sides and bottom of the lining. Do not turn the lining.

3 Attach the lining: Place the bag inside the lining. Line up the top edges and stitch around the top of the bag, leaving an opening for turning. Turn the bag right side out through the opening and press. Push the lining into place inside the bag and press.

4 Make the handles: Place a 3" x 18" pink strip right-side-up on your work surface. Top with a 3" x 18" ivory strip right-side-down. Stitch around the edges, leaving an opening for turning. Turn and press. Hand stitch the opening closed. Repeat, for a total of two handles.

5 Attach the handles: Attach a handle to each side of the tote bag, referring to the photo for placement. Hand stitch buttons to the ends of each handle.

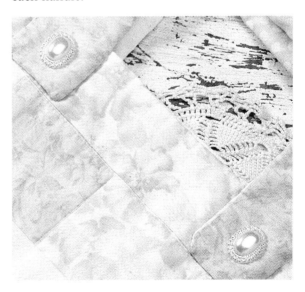

Cell Phone Case

I used a scrap snipped from an old floral bedspread to make this fast and easy cell phone case. Using a bedspread for this project adds enough padding and weight to protect your cell phone from damage. You can also use this case for your reading or sunglasses.

You will need:

Vintage linens
* scrap from a floral bedspread, at least 10" x 10"
* scrap of cotton to match the bedspread, at least 10" x 10"

Other fabric and trims
* gold and ivory filigree button, ½" diameter

Other supplies
* rotary cutter, ruler, and mat, or ruler, fabric marker, and scissors
* needle and thread
* sewing machine and accessories (this project can be done by hand, but it will be more time-consuming)
* iron and pressing surface

Directions

Note: This project uses a ¼" seam allowance.

1 Cut the fabrics:

From the bedspread cut:
7½" x 7½" square

From the matching cotton cut:
7½" x 7½" square

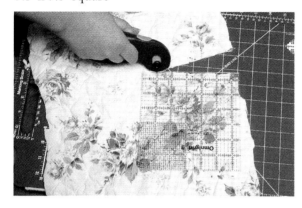

2 Place the bedspread square and the matching cotton with the right sides together, lining up the edges. Stitch around the edges of the square, leaving an opening for turning.

3 Turn and press. Hand stitch the opening closed.

4 Fold the square in half, with the bedspread side facing in. Stitch across the bottom and up the side of the case, stopping 2" from the top.

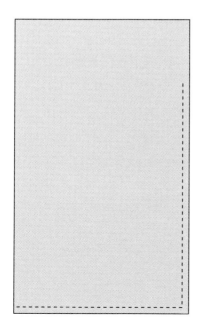

5 Turn the case so the right side (bedspread side) is facing out. Press.

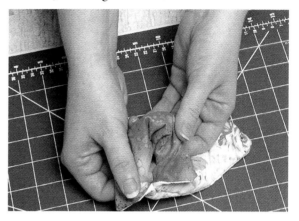

6 Choose the most attractive side of the case for the front and fold it down to form a flap. Press.

7 Hand stitch a button to the folded flap, stitching through both the folded portion and the front of the case. This will keep the flap in place.

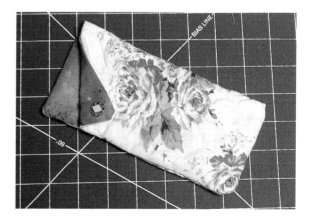

Covered Buttons

Even the tiniest scraps can be used for projects. Cover buttons with embroidered motifs from leftover or damaged pieces. The finished buttons can be used on clothing or for home décor projects.

Directions

1 Select an embroidered scrap and place it right-side-up on your pressing surface. Iron the scrap to remove any wrinkles.

2 Place the rounded disk portion of the button on top of the scrap and use the water-soluble marker to draw a circle around the button, ½" from the edge. The circle doesn't have to be perfect – the edges won't show in the finished product.

3 Use scissors to cut the embroidered scrap on the marked line.

4 With the wrong side up, place the fabric over the button maker.

You will need:

Vintage linens
* assorted scraps with embroidered motifs

Other supplies
* ¾" and 1½" buttons to cover (I used the Cover Buttons kit by Prym, which includes all the tools)
* scissors
* water-soluble fabric marker
* iron and pressing surface

6 With the shank side up, place the button back into the button maker. Use the pusher to snap the button in place.

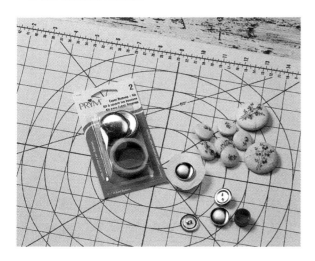

5 Use the rounded disk portion of the button to push the fabric into the button maker (the rounded portion of the button will snap into place). Tuck the fabric edges over the back of the button.

Scrap Ornaments

These scrappy ornaments make up in a flash. Use them on your Christmas tree or to accent wrapped packages. A set of ornaments would make a great holiday hostess gift.

Directions

1 Make a plastic template: Use a pencil to trace the Star pattern from page 128 onto the clear plastic template sheet. Cut out the star template.

2 Stitch together random scraps of fabric to make a 7" pieced square. After piecing, sew additional scraps with trims on top of the square as desired.

3 Place the chenille scrap with the right side down on a flat work surface. Spray with a light coat of fabric basting spray and top with the pieced square, right-side-up. Press the fabrics together.

4 Place the clear plastic star template on top of the pieced square. Move the template around until you are happy with the way the cut piece will look. (Experiment with different areas of the square until you find one you like.) Trace around the star template with a water-soluble fabric marker.

5 Stitch on the marked line all the way around the star. Use scissors to trim the fabric around the star ¼" away from the stitched line.

6 Use scissors to snip the seam allowances all the way around the star. Snip up to, but not over the stitching line. Wash and dry the star.

7 Stuff the star with fiberfill and hand stitch the opening closed.

8 Fold the metallic gold embroidery floss in half to form a loop. Knot the ends and hand stitch the floss in place on the back of the star for a hanger.

You will need:

Vintage linens
* assorted scraps, ⅛ yard total
* scrap of chenille for ornament back, at least 7" x 7"

Trim
* 12" length of metallic gold embroidery floss

Other supplies
* clear plastic template sheet
* pencil
* water-soluble fabric marker
* fabric basting spray
* fiberfill
* scissors
* sewing machine and accessories (this project can be done by hand, but it will be more time-consuming)
* needle and thread

To make this version, piece the ornament front with scraps from men's clothing and ties and stitch them together with metallic gold thread. Assemble as directed.

Woven Seat Chair

Use large leftover scraps from cotton bedspreads, curtains, sheets, tablecloths, and other home furnishings to get the long strips for this project. I found this chair at a garage sale for $3. The wood frame on this type of chair holds up much better than the original caned seat. "Seatless" chairs are very easy and inexpensive to find. If you can't find one without a seat, use scissors to remove the cane seat and proceed as directed.

Directions

1 Paint the chair: Use the foam brush to paint the chair with white satin finish paint. Let the paint dry. If your chair is a dark color, apply a second coat of white paint and let it dry.

2 Tear the fabric scraps into 2" wide strips. If you are using a fabric that doesn't tear easily, use a rotary cutter or scissors. The strips don't need to be perfect and the ragged edges will enhance the look of the finished seat.

3 With the chair facing you, tie the end of one fabric strip (any color) to the back seat supports. Tie another fabric strip to the first strip, forming a fabric chain. Do not trim the tails of the resulting knot – these loose ends form the fringe below the seat.

4 Add the vertical strips: Wrap the fabric strip chain over the front seat support. Continue wrapping the fabric chain around the front and back seat supports. Add strips of fabric to your fabric chain as needed until the chair seat is completely covered. Finish the vertical strips by tying the fabric to the back seat support.

You will need:

Vintage linens
* large scraps of leftover cotton fabrics, about 2 yards total

Other supplies
* ladder-back chair without a seat
* plant mister filled with water
* satin finish paint in white (I used Soft White Americana Satin by DecoArt)
* acrylic craft paint in white, blue, pink, green, and yellow (I used White Wash, Blue Chiffon, Baby Pink, Silver Sage Green, and Pineapple by DecoArt)
* 1" foam paintbrush
* 1" old scruffy paintbrush
* ½" flat brush
* liner brush
* plastic plate or palette
* paper towels
* rotary cutter, ruler, and mat, or ruler, fabric marker, and scissors
* pencil

5 With the chair facing you, tie the end of one fabric strip (any color) to one of the side seat supports. Begin weaving the horizontal rows with a simple over-and-under basket weave pattern. Weave under the first vertical band of fabric and over the next. Continue across in this fashion until you reach the opposite seat support. Wrap the fabric chain around the support and weave in the opposite direction. Continue weaving, adding fabric strips as needed, and allowing the knotted ends to hang below the seat. Use firm pressure when weaving, but don't stretch the fabric.

6 When the horizontal rows are complete, tie the end of the fabric chain to the back seat support to secure. Push any knots of ends that are on top of the seat underneath. Mist the finished seat lightly with water and let it dry. The fabric will tighten up slightly as it dries.

Paint the Front and Back of the Chair Slats

1 For the top slat, pour pink paint on a plastic plate or palette and add water to thin the paint slightly. Use the scruffy brush to apply the paint to the slat, using a pouncing motion. Blot the wet paint with a paper towel, creating a mottled finish. Let the paint dry. Using a liner brush, paint thin wavy diagonal stripes of white in one direction. Overlap with a second set of stripes in the other direction. Let the paint dry.

2 Paint the second slat with green and let the paint dry. Use a brush handle to add dots of white. Let the paint dry.

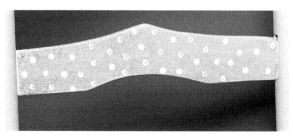

3 For the third slat, pour blue paint on a plastic plate or palette and add water to thin the paint slightly. Use the scruffy brush to apply the paint to the slat, using a pouncing motion. Blot the wet paint with a paper towel, creating a mottled finish. Let the paint dry. Use a ½" flat brush to add vertical stripes of white. Let the paint dry.

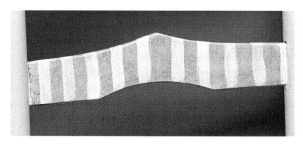

4 Paint the bottom slat with yellow paint and let the paint dry. Use the liner brush to add coils of white. Let the paint dry.

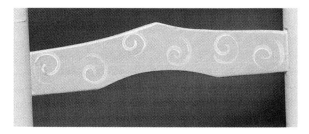

Chapter 6

Crafting Techniques

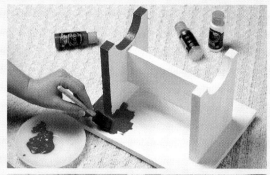

Painting

The projects in this book require a minimal amount of painting. You will need paint in the appropriate colors, disposable foam brushes, and a few small brushes for detail work. The surfaces won't require much preparation and all of the projects have distressed finishes, so less-than-perfect surfaces will only add to their charm. Be sure that the surfaces are clean and ready to accept paint. If the surface has a very shiny finish, sand it lightly before beginning.

Most painted surfaces can be painted over with acrylic or latex paints. Sand the finish lightly so the new paint will adhere and proceed as directed. Avoid sanding surfaces with lead painted finishes. Instead, paint directly over the original finish or use a different piece entirely. Never use lead painted pieces in a child's or baby's room.

Photo Transfer

There are two basic methods and products for transferring photos and text to fabric. Both methods create clear, attractive copies of your photos, so choose the one that is most convenient for you. The photos used for the projects in this book were scanned, edited with computer software, then printed out on an inkjet printer. I used Duncan's Tulip Iron-on Transfer Paper for Color Inkjet Printers.

Transferring Photos and Text Using a Color Copier

Take your photo and/or printed text to a copy center and have it copied onto a sheet of transfer paper. You will need to supply the transfer paper. Copy centers occasionally stock transfer paper, but it is not usually the best quality. You can use the color copier to edit your design as needed (make it smaller or larger, adjust the color, or use other special features). Be sure to choose the "mirror image" function when transferring text. The print will look backwards on your copy but will be legible when ironed onto fabric. Use this method if you don't have access to a computer and printer, or if you are in a hurry (a color copier will print out your transfer sheet in under a minute).

Transferring Photos and Text Using a Computer and Printer

Use a digital camera or scanner to capture images, then print your photo onto transfer paper. You can use the computer to edit your design as needed (make it smaller or larger, adjust the color, or use other special features). Be sure to choose the "mirror image" function when transferring text. The print will look backwards on your printout but will be legible when ironed onto fabric.

Use this method if you have access to a computer and inkjet printer and want the convenience of editing and printing without leaving the house. Transfers created using this method need to dry completely before they can be used, so allow a little extra time for printing and drying.

Both Methods

Follow the manufacturer's directions to transfer the photo to the fabric. You will need an iron and a pressing surface. For best results, transfer your images to high quality, 100% cotton white fabric. Never touch the transferred images with a hot iron, as they will smear or melt.

Aging New Fabrics

As you consider doing the projects in this book, you may find that you can't locate the perfect match for one of your vintage pieces, or that you don't have quite enough fabric to complete a project. Thanks to the popularity of the vintage look, there are many reproduction fabrics available today. Traditional fabrics can often be aged as well, making them suitable for your vintage linens projects. Try one of the techniques that follow to add instant age to a new or reproduction fabric.

For all of the methods, wash and dry the new fabric prior to aging to remove any sizing on the surface of the fabric. Wash again after the aging is complete to be sure all of the solutions you used are out of the fabric. Store artificially-aged fabrics with your vintage linens until you are ready to use them.

To age fabric, you need to either add color using natural or artificial dyes, or remove color by fading the fabric. Additive techniques include tea or coffee dying, cola staining, or using commercial dye products. Subtractive techniques include sun fading, bleaching, and reversing the fabric (using the "wrong" side).

You can also alter the appearance of some fabrics, like wool and silk, by felting. You can make your own felted wool using your washer and dryer. Visit a thrift shop or resale shop and purchase a few 100% wool pieces. Pants, skirts, sweaters, and suit jackets come in a variety of colors and provide a good amount of fabric to work with.

To felt a piece, first remove the lining and tags, then wash the piece in hot water with detergent but no fabric softener. Dry in the dryer at the cotton or permanent press setting. Remove from the dryer and use as desired. This technique results in thick, textured wool that can be used in a variety of projects.

Coffee and Tea Dying

Coffee and tea dying use the same basic method to infuse fabric with a sheer wash of color. The finished results vary only in color and intensity. Tinting your fabric with coffee produces a deep, warm tan that is ideal for primitive, masculine, or very antique looking projects. Tea dying produces a more subtle ivory hue and works well for light and delicate colors, and when a slight patina of age is needed.

You will need:

* large soup pot or Dutch oven
* 5 teabags or ½ cup instant coffee
* fabric (up to 1 yard)
* scissors

Directions

1 Fill the large soup pot or Dutch oven about halfway with water and bring it to a boil. Add the instant coffee or teabags and turn off the heat. Let the brew steep for 10 minutes.

2 While the tea or coffee is steeping, cut a test swatch from your fabric. Add the test swatch to the pot and let it soak for 10 minutes. Use tongs or a fork to remove the test swatch from the pot. Rinse the swatch at the sink until the water runs clear and check the color. The fabric will look slightly lighter when it is dry. If the fabric is too dark, cut another swatch and soak it for five minutes, then rinse and test the color. If the test fabric is too light, return it to the pot. Rinse the swatch and check the color every 10 minutes until you are happy with the color.

3 Once you are happy with the color of the test swatch, add the fabric to the pot and let it soak for the number of minutes that gives you the result you want, then remove it. Rinse the fabric in the sink, wring it out, then let it air dry. Press with a warm iron to set the color.

Cola Staining

Cola staining produces a warm, reddish tint. I discovered this technique by accident, after spilling a can of soda on a pile of linens waiting to be washed. After discovering the mess, I tried to wash out the soda. It didn't come out, but the resulting stains were a beautiful color! Be sure to wash your cola-stained fabrics in the washer after dying them. The sugar in the soda will attract pests and could damage the fibers of your fabric.

You will need:

* plastic bucket
* (2) 2 liter containers of cola, any brand
* fabric (up to 1 yard)

Directions

1 Pour both bottles of soda into the bucket and add the fabric.

2 Let the fabric soak for 30 minutes, then rinse it under cool running water. If the color is dark enough, immediately wash and dry it. If the fabric is not dark enough, return it to the bucket. Check the fabric every 10 minutes until you are satisfied with the color. Discard the soda when done.

Sun Fading

Some fabrics will fade easily in the sun, others will not. The only way to know for sure which fabrics will work is to try them. Sun fading won't damage your fabrics, so don't be afraid to experiment. Sun fading will not work on acrylics, polyester blends, or rayon.

You will need:

* water
* fabric (up to 1 yard)
* plastic tablecloth
* scissors

Directions

1 On a bright, sunny morning, place a plastic tablecloth on a flat, clean surface in direct sunlight outdoors. Cut a swatch from the fabric and set it aside.

2 Thoroughly wet the remaining fabric and wring it out. Spread the fabric out on top of the tablecloth with the right side up. If it is a very windy day, weigh the corners of the fabric down with pattern weights or small clean rocks.

3 Let the fabric bake in the sun for several hours. When the fabric is dry, compare it to the swatch. If the fabric has faded, repeat the process until the desired look is achieved. If there has been no change, use one of the bleaching methods described below.

Bleaching

Bleaching can produce either extreme or mild fading, or ruin your fabric entirely. Handle bleach with care and never pour it directly on fabric. For slight-to-moderate fading on most types of fabric, use a bleach mist technique. Misting allows you to apply diluted bleach to the surface of the fabric, resulting in an even faded tone.

You will need:

* bleach
* plant or hair mister
* permanent black marker
* water
* fabric (up to 1 yard)
* plastic tablecloth

Directions

1 Place a plastic tablecloth on a flat, clean surface in direct sunlight outdoors.

2 Thoroughly wet the fabric and wring it out. Spread the fabric out on top of the tablecloth with the right side up. If it is a very windy day, weigh the corners of the fabric down with pattern weights or small clean rocks.

3 Use the marker to label the mister bottle. Once you have used it for bleaching, you will not want to use it on plants or your hair! Carefully pour bleach into the bottle until it is about one quarter full. Fill the bottle with water. Add the lid and shake the bottle to combine the bleach and water. Mist the fabric thoroughly with the bleach mixture.

4 For mild fading, let the fabric dry in the shade. For more fading, let the fabric dry in the sun. Check the fabric after an hour to be sure it has not faded too much. When fabric has faded to a color you like, wash and dry it immediately to stop the bleaching process.

Bleaching in the Washer

Bleach your fabrics in the washer if you want a lot of fading or if the weather is inclement. Fill the washer with hot water and add 1 cup of bleach. Let the washer agitate for a minute to blend. Do not add detergent. Add the fabrics you wish to bleach and let the washer agitate until all the fabrics are saturated. Let the fabrics soak for an hour, then let the washer complete the cycle. When the wash cycle is compete, run the washer a second time, this time with detergent, to rinse away any lingering bleach. Dry the fabric in the dryer.

Quilting

Complete the quilt top as directed. Choose a backing fabric and piece the back if needed. Place the quilt back on a flat work surface and smooth out any wrinkles. Spray the back with a light coat of basting spray and top it with quilt batting. Smooth out the quilt batting. Spray the batting with a light coat of basting spray and top it with the quilt front. Smooth the quilt top. Hand or machine quilt as desired. Refer to a good quilting book for information on quilting techniques.

About the Author

Samantha McNesby first became interested in creating projects using authentic vintage linens after attending a large quilt show in Lancaster, Pennsylvania in 1998. This was the first large show she had ever attended and she was drawn to the booths that sold old quilts, trims, and vintage fabrics. Very few exhibitors featured anything made with these scraps – and they were often relegated to a bin in the back of the booth. Samantha was determined to find a use for the wonderful pieces she brought home from that show.

As she created more and more designs for new projects using vintage items, she began to explore auctions, flea markets, and yard sales and later discovered thrift shops, where she can spend hours looking at old clothing and linens. She has found that shopping for old linens is just as fun as making projects with them!

As a designer for the creative services industry, Samantha works on a variety of projects each year. Her favorites are the ones that feature vintage linens, trims, and other "old" items. Samantha loves shopping for, handling, and using these objects and will often purchase an item with no particular project in mind, simply because it's beautiful or interesting.

Samantha is the author of several painting and crafting leaflets and her projects are regularly featured in national crafting and home décor magazines.

Resources

Paints and Mediums
DecoArt
Stanford, KY 40484
(800) 367-3047
www.decoart.com

Transfer Paper
Duncan
5673 E. Shields Ave.
Fresno, CA 93727
(800) 438-6226
www.duncancrafts.com
*Tulip Iron-on Transfer Paper for Color Copiers,
Tulip Iron-on Transfer Paper for Inkjet Printers*

Glue
Beacon Adhesives
Mt. Vernon, NY 10550
(914) 699-3400
www.beaconcreates.com
Gem-Tac Glue

Quilting
Island Threads
10225 Ocean Hwy. 17
Pawleys Island, SC 29585
(843) 235-3725
ithreads@sccoast.net
*The quilts in this book were professionally quilted
by Pat Roman, owner.*

Internet Resources
www.ebay.com
*The world's largest online auction site is very user-
friendly and includes easy-to-use tutorials.*

www.BlueBearBeads.com
*My favorite bead and button shop. The vintage
buttons in the projects were purchased here.*

www.cocochenille.com
*Great selection of chenille, from scrap bags to full-
sized bedspreads.*

www.reprodepotfabrics.com
*Huge selection of vintage and new fabrics, clothing,
and trims, sorted by era and type.*

Patterns

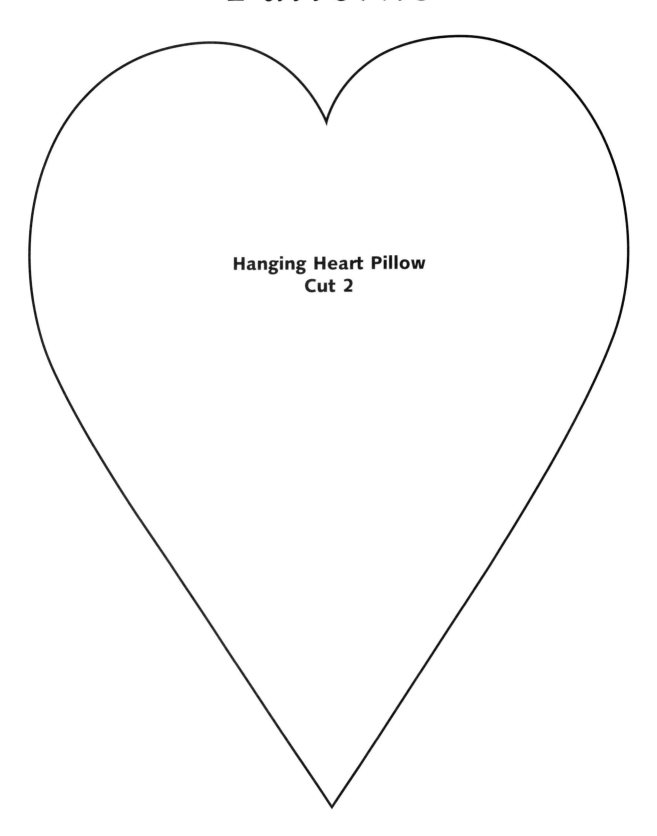

**Hanging Heart Pillow
Cut 2**

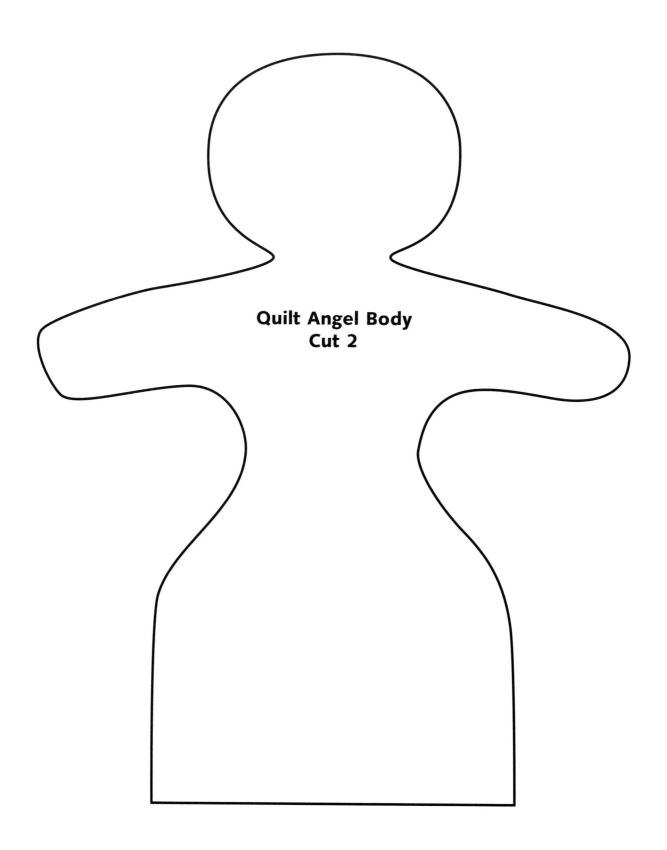

**Quilt Angel Body
Cut 2**

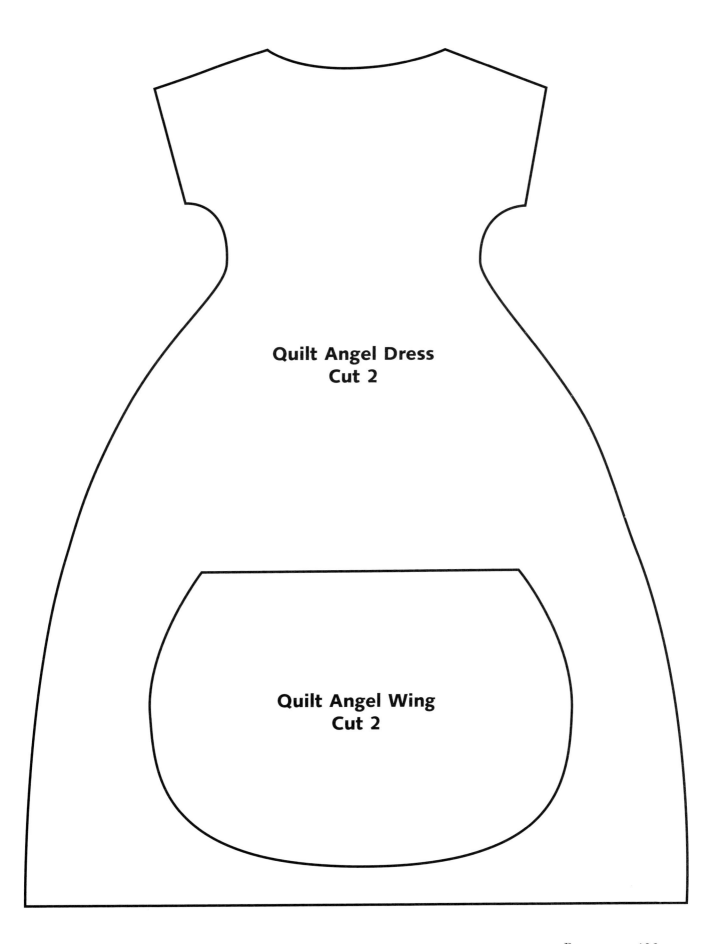

Quilt Angel Dress
Cut 2

Quilt Angel Wing
Cut 2

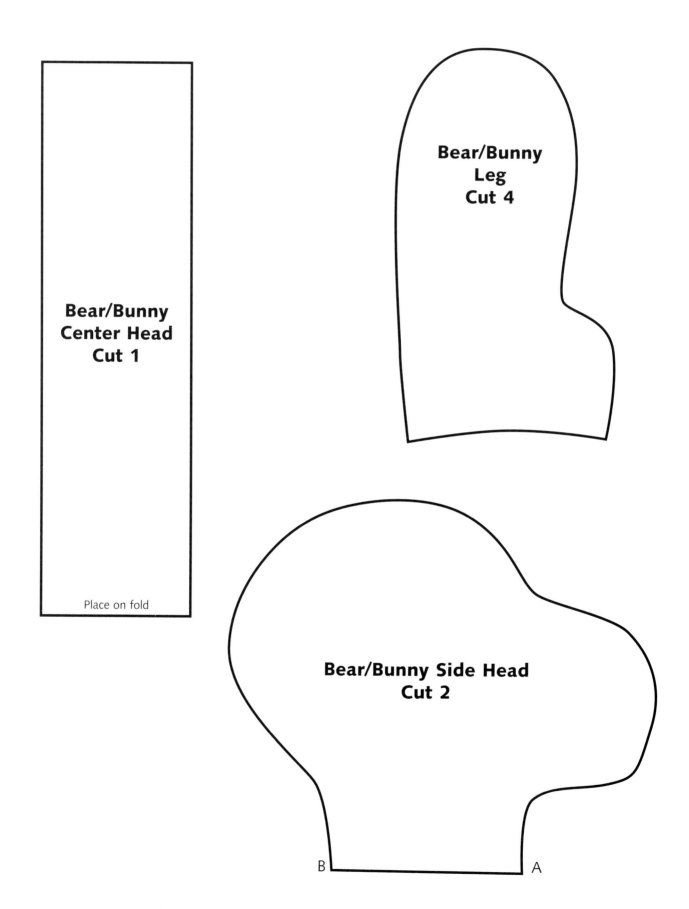

**Bear/Bunny
Leg
Cut 4**

**Bear/Bunny
Center Head
Cut 1**

Place on fold

**Bear/Bunny Side Head
Cut 2**

B   A

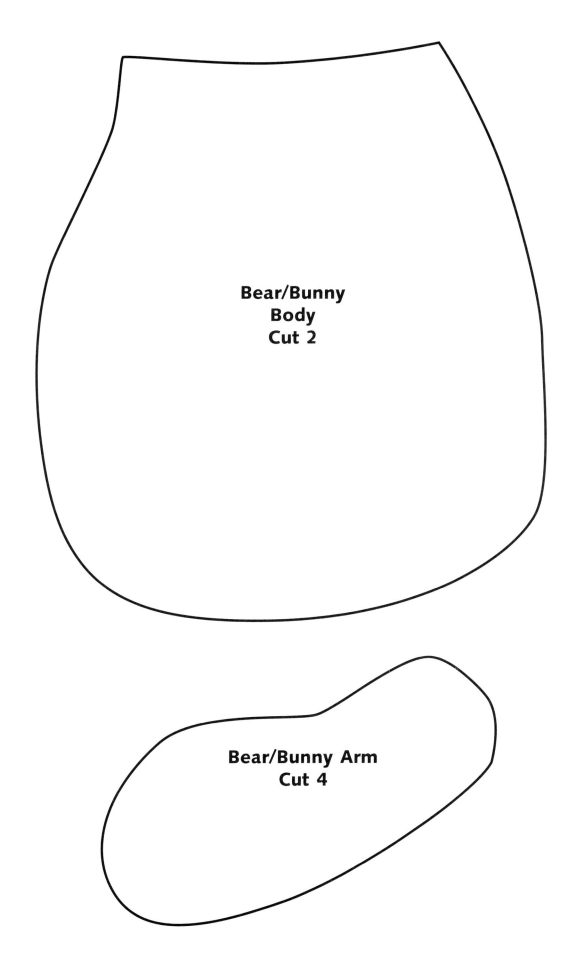

**Bear/Bunny
Body
Cut 2**

**Bear/Bunny Arm
Cut 4**

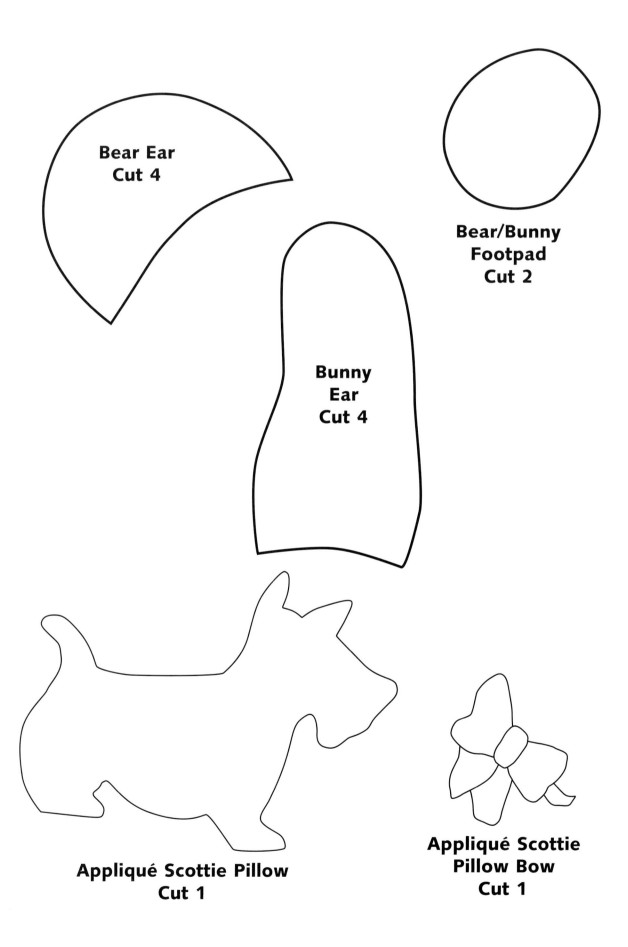

Bear Ear
Cut 4

Bear/Bunny
Footpad
Cut 2

Bunny
Ear
Cut 4

Appliqué Scottie Pillow
Cut 1

Appliqué Scottie
Pillow Bow
Cut 1

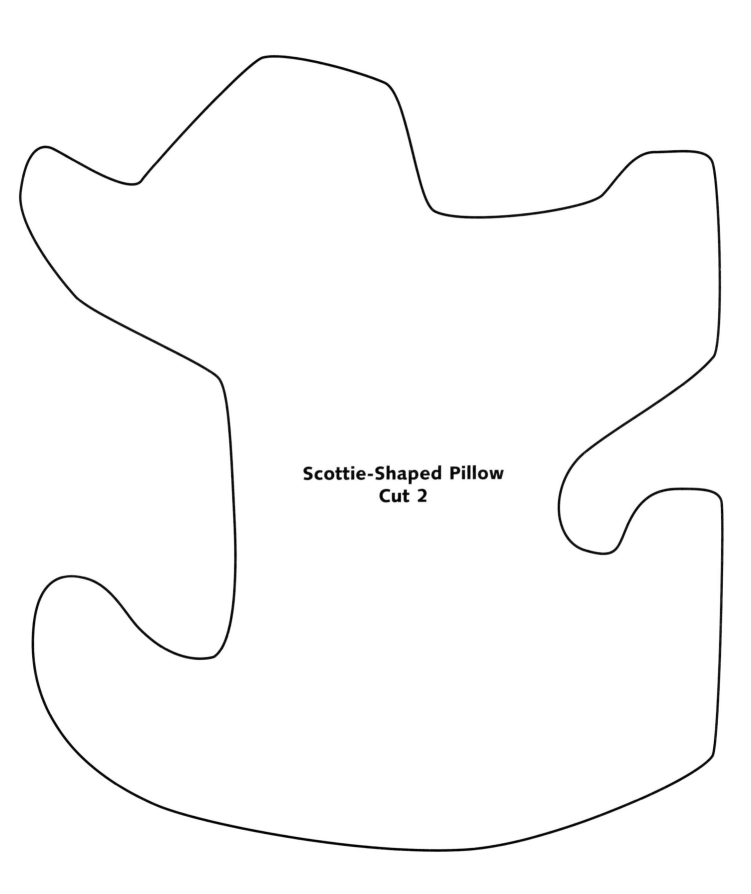

**Scottie-Shaped Pillow
Cut 2**

Star Ornament
Cut 1 from pieced scraps
Cut 1 from chenille